In *Dress With Style,* Joanne Wallace has the practical solutions that will allow you to become the attractive woman God intended you to be. You'll be able to:

- Become a wise, economically minded shopper
- Select outfits for church functions, job interviews, dinner parties, and other occasions
- Help the man in your life to look his best
- Minimize figure flaws and emphasize assets
- Select colors that complement your natural coloring
- Learn many more keys to self-improvement

Only God can make you beautiful within—but *Dress With Style* can teach you how to let that beauty come out.

Dress With Style

BY JOANNE WALLACE
The Image of Loveliness
Dress With Style

DRESS
with
STYLE

Joanne Wallace

Fleming H. Revell Company
Old Tappan, New Jersey

Library of Congress Cataloging in Publication Data
Wallace, Joanne.
    Dress with style.
    1. Clothing and dress.   2. Fashion.   I. Title.
TT507.W215   1982   646'.34   82-11276
ISBN 0-8007-1313-3

TO my mother,
Mary Gibson,
who from the day I was born
taught me good grooming principles

Contents

Acknowledgments

To Marge Nelson and my daughter, Deanna Early, who diligently edited and typed the manuscript

To my husband, Jim, and my son, Bob, who were a constant encouragement

To David Morris, my photographer

To the beautiful models: Denise Nelson, Barbara Ross, Debi Wyant, Bonnie Hoerner, Jill Siegmund, Hope Bulgin, Cathy Dotson, Nancy Kleiver, and Jan Brehm

Illustrations by Sherry La Munyan

Preface

For years, many women who were raised in the church atmosphere have looked upon outward beauty as vanity.

Dr. John Graham, a Christian and well-known plastic surgeon, shared with me the true meaning of the word *vanity* while appearing on my weekly television program. "The word *vanity* comes from a Greek word which means 'emptiness' or 'without purpose.'" The question then is whether or not being well dressed, well groomed, and wanting to look attractive is "empty or without purpose."

Women have every right to show concern for their outward appearance, if it is done with purpose and meaning.

Women are created in the image of God and are His handiwork. It is for this reason, if for no other, that you present yourself in the best way possible and keep this gift—your body—attractive. I do not believe that God's creations should be haggard, drab, or dowdy. Nor do I believe they should appear cheap, tasteless, or immodest. Quite the contrary! God created the beauty of sunsets, daffodils, the splendor of the autumn leaves falling in radiant color— and *you*, His most lovely creation of all!

When people meet for the first time, an impression is left—if it is pleasing, there will be further contact. If it is displeasing, it can mean the end of a potential friendship.

At times, appearance can lead to the disintegration of a well-established relationship. My file is overflowing with letters from women who confide that they neglected their outward appearance, which was a factor that led to their husbands' being unfaithful. One woman wrote, "After reading *The Image of Loveliness*, I realized how I had neglected myself and saw myself as the foolish woman of Proverbs 14:1. 'A wise woman builds her house, while a foolish woman tears hers down by her own efforts.'" Your body can be thought of as your "house."

My purpose is to present you with a simple, practical, and educational book of workable, functional clothing and dressing tips to help you be a good steward and a good representative. The literature in this field is abundant, but it is widely scattered. Hence, I have tried to give you precise information all in one book, while also reflecting a personal view.

You are a custom-made individual, created unique with your very own beautiful color palette of hair, eyes, and skin tone, designed with your own physical frame, and ready to develop your own personal style.

JOANNE WALLACE

Dress With Style

The Language of Dress

A beautiful woman lacking discretion and modesty is like a fine gold ring in a pig's snout.
Proverbs 11:22

Do you realize that you never have a second chance to make a good first impression?

While I was conducting a seminar for seminary students on good grooming and appearance, a young interning minister said, "The truth is, I don't have time to look good. I'm too busy."

Well, usually the busier we are, the more visible we become. It is even more important, therefore, that we take the time and make the extra effort to look good.

It is a proven fact that the people who look successful are given better service in public places than those who do not.

Try it yourself: Go shopping in jeans sometime, and then return the next day dressed in a suit.

My son, Bob, home one summer after his sophomore year of college, went to town to purchase some new clothing with one hundred dollars of his hard-earned money. He wore his usual school jeans and shirt to go shopping. He waited, but no salesperson came to help him. Frustrated and upset, he left the store and came home. He asked himself, *Would it have made any difference if I'd dressed differently?*

Bob decided to experiment. The next morning he put on a nice pair of slacks, blazer, shirt, and tie. He returned to the same store, at the same time, when the same salespeople were present. Within seconds he had a salesperson's attention, and quickly spent his one hundred dollars (and made additional purchases on Mom's charge account!).

Nonverbal Communication

Through Clothing

If you are skeptical about the impact clothes have on your life, consider how television producers use clothes to establish a character on a show.

Since air time is limited, what a character wears helps to very quickly identify that personality. Producers consider clothes so crucial that they continually confer with wardrobe people to discuss each "look."

Prior to each of my weekly television shows (which are nationally syndicated), I very carefully plan what I will wear. I know how important it is to immediately establish who I am, and the message that I wish to convey, by what I wear.

In our society, certain "looks" have specific meanings. This may not seem fair, but it is a reality! A case in point is a woman's hairstyle. The general concensus is that long hair is more sensuous, that blonds have more fun, and that gray hair on a woman (no matter how beautiful she may be) makes her look old! On the other hand, gray hair on a man is thought to be distinguished. It's not fair!

Shampoo commercials feature models with volumes of gorgeous hair. Advertisements for household products focus on shorter, thinner-haired women.

Charlene Tilton (Lucy of "Dallas") may make millions of dollars with her long, blond, sun-streaked hair, but it is difficult for me to picture her in the role of an administrative assistant.

There is just no getting around the fact that you are often judged by your appearance, and that happens before you ever have a chance to speak. First impressions are made in a very short time, often as short as ten seconds!

Many psychotherapists agree that close to 90 percent of what people remember is through nonverbal communication: body language and facial expressions. Hair, posture, clothes, and skin are the keys. Often only about 10 percent of what you say is remembered.

This doesn't mean that we should all look like big-city executives. Where we live, our age, and the kind of work we do should affect how we dress.

Besides being a great spiritual teacher, my pastor is a very loving, kind, and "real" person. He always looks the part of a minister. I never find myself questioning his authority or honesty. I believe this is partly because he always looks and acts the part of a minister, both on and off the platform. I believe his clothing has something to do with his authoritative demeanor and his credibility.

What You're Saying Through

Your Public Image

Have you ever spent time watching people at an airport? Maybe you've noticed the woman in a hurry who pushes her way to the boarding gate. Noting her clothing or hairstyle, you may have thought, *What a bossy person. And her makeup looks like a Halloween mask!* Or maybe, *She's a mess. She probably left the house with curlers in her hair and took them out on the way.*

Snap judgments. We're all guilty of them at one time or another. The sad thing is, these mental impressions are often lasting—even when they are wrong.

For better or worse, we need to realize that our outward appearance influences how other people will react to us. Add voice, posture, hairstyle, makeup, wardrobe, and what you are carrying or reading, and you'll discover what your public image is.

What does *your* image say? Unfortunately, most of us have difficulty being objective about how we look. But it is important to at least determine what you *think* you're portraying to the outside world.

I know a woman who always wears tight dresses with slits that extend to her hips. Perhaps she only wants to convey the message that she is "fun, confident, and attractive." But when the message is received and decoded it may read, "I'm available. Your place or mine?" Sometimes this type of woman is searching, in the only way she knows how, for love and affection.

A person with a dingy, sloppy appearance, messy hair, and ungroomed clothes may be saying, "I don't care." People often avoid her because she carries an aura of dejection that is depressing to those around her.

Now, I realize that we all look "grungy" once in a while; but if this is your *typical* attire, you may want to determine the subconscious reasons behind your clothes choices.

Perhaps you need new friends, new interests, or a new job. Try finding a new interest, and your life and looks will be better for it!

Susie took our eight-week course in image building. She began to long for a change in herself that would attract new friends. Through the Image Improvement program, she began to see that *she* was responsible for her own life—no one else. She began to change her exterior image from that of a rigid, uptight suit and matronly hairstyle to a soft, feminine, yet very professional look. Through a local church, she joined a singles group where she met new friends, and took a class at the community college to prepare her for a new future, new interests, and a new job!

We all present ourselves in different ways under different circumstances. The way we dress for church, the grocery store, and social dinners all reflect our feelings about ourselves. Study how you dress under pressure (for a job interview or a party). This can tell you how tense you are about the event, and perhaps reveal your pattern for handling or mishandling stress. If you're going to a party, do you dress drably and without originality so no one will notice you? Or do you dress in such a bizarre fashion that you cannot help being noticed?

The way you dress tells so much about your self-image and self-esteem. Hopefully, the way you see yourself on the inside is positive and will also be the way the world views you.

You Can Get Your Clothes

to Say What You Want

Every day you send messages by the clothes you wear.

Here are some hints to help you look great regardless of the occasion. Study the message each one conveys.

It's not necessary to always follow the rule for wearing a business "uniform." Wear a jacket and skirt with feminine touches. Be certain the fabric is quality material and that the fit is perfect.

Take a look at what she is wearing:

Occasion A business appointment, a job interview, a speaking engagement.

Nonverbal Language "You can count on me! I am dependable. I can do it. Listen to me!"

Unspoken Response "You are the one! You're hired! We believe you!"

The Image Professional and businesslike. The suit elicits respect. Your personality shows through.

Wear casual pants, a comfortable top, some up-to-date accessories, and presto! You'll look terrific!

Take a look at what she is wearing:

Occasion Relaxing on a trip to the lake; family-fun activities.

Nonverbal Language "I can be casual and still look wonderful!"

Unspoken Response "You look so comfortable and yet so fashionable."

The Image Your individuality shows—the real you. Your look is restful and pleasing, as though it didn't require a great deal of work to prepare.

When you are in an informal situation where you will be seated most of the time, it is important to place your fashion emphasis on the upper torso, especially when communicating from behind a table.

Take a look at what she is wearing:

Occasion A PTA meeting, a club luncheon, an afternoon tea with old friends.

Nonverbal Language "I feel wonderful! This is the best time of my life!"

Unspoken Response "You're looking better all the time."

The Image You have the attention-getting look that this situation calls for, yet you are tastefully and appropriately dressed.

The "hostess" look gives the message that you're feminine and approachable. It sets the mood for a memorable night.

Take a look at what she is wearing:

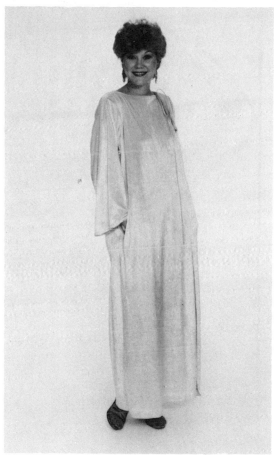

Occasion A dinner party, a candlelight dinner, hostessing responsibility, or a special evening at home.

Nonverbal Language "Tonight I want to look especially beautiful."

Spoken Response "Honey, you look gorgeous!"

The Image The way you look tonight will bring compliments. The clothes you wear are sending a message for this very special evening. Yes, your man loves you just as you are, but how nice it is to occasionally wear something special at home just for him.

What Is Your Clothing Personality?

Timely advice is as lovely as golden apples in a silver basket.

Proverbs 25:11

Have you ever been to a style show? If your answer is yes, I'd like you to think again. I don't believe any of us have been to a *style* show—only a *fashion* show. Style, you see, is a very personal part of us that cannot be easily defined. True personal style can be elusive.

Finding your own personal style means understanding who you are. Age has nothing to do with this, as your unique personal style is one that lasts a lifetime. You are an original. Recognize this, and be happy.

Most women have an innate sense of what looks good on them—and what doesn't. Every woman needs to concentrate on looking good within her own style.

Fashion presents us with many different types of styles. Let's look at a few to see if you can identify yourself. You may find that more than one type fits you. For example, you may be the sporty type on weekends, the romantic type in the evenings, and the classic type for work.

What's Your Style?

Sophisticated Are your ambitions high? Do you dream of driving a sports car, being the company president, or traveling around the world? Do you enter a room with an air of elegance?

You're a sophisticate, one who coordinates her wardrobe carefully, shopping for sales on designer clothes. You have a distinct way of dressing, no matter what the occasion. You cause heads to turn, and you're not afraid to try something new.

Romantic   Do you adore old movies, poetry, and love songs? Do you remember every anniversary, and melt in candlelight and soft music?

You're the romantic who loves looking feminine and pretty. You'd much rather wear a dress than pants. Your tastes run to ruffles and lace, pastels and whites. Anything nostalgic, dainty, and soft appeals to you.

Sporty   Do you run when you could be walking? Love the outdoor life? Do you keep your roller skates at the front door? Do you relish the thought of waking early, greeting every day with a smile?

You're the sporty type who likes comfortable, versatile, and practical clothes. You probably prefer shorts or pants to a dress, and insist on loose-fitting, wash-and-wear fabrics. You prefer clothes with flair and movement—just like your activities!

Classic   Are you highly organized? Outgoing and loyal? Do you attend all high-school reunions and keep in touch with old friends?

You're the classic type. You prefer tailored clothes, and love working with separates. You're interested in getting the maximum wear out of your clothes and go for durable, seasonless styles.

Daring   Are you the first to try a new fashion? Do you find yourself leading instead of following? Do you love debating just for the sake of debating? Do fast cars, safaris, and deep-sea diving trips sound appealing?

You're the individualist who dares to wear unlikely combinations—and who looks great! You have a unique style. No one does it quite like you.

To Help You Improve Your Image, Consider the Following

How do you look in your daydreams? Are you soft and feminine in those dreams, but tailored and conservative in real life? If you would like to look different, concentrate on the things that will make the change. Would a new hairstyle or a different cosmetic portray your new look?

Analyze why you look the way you do. What has caused you to develop your particular look? Do you avoid jewelry because your mother told you it was "frivolous adornment"? Do you wear the same hairstyle because it was the one you wore when you met your husband fifteen years ago?

Analyze the messages you get from other people. Do they treat you as though you are younger or older than you are? Do they say, "Don't worry your pretty little head," when you really want to talk seriously? Write down the reactions you get to particular styles you wear.

Find your goal in life. Do you want a new job or a promotion with the same company? Perhaps your image should be more confident and businesslike. If you desire a more active social life, perhaps your clothing (when you are with friends) should be more relaxed and casual.

Pay attention to the outfits you feel best in. What is there about them that makes you feel so good? Ask yourself why you dislike certain garments. Write down your answers. They will help you understand and define your own image and unique style.

How to Choose the Right Clothes for You

How many times have you looked into your bulging closet and said, "I don't have a thing to wear"? If you've said this, you may need help from some very important guidelines. When you buy clothing, it's important to select items that enhance your *life-style,* your *job,* and *you!* Possibly you have been following fashion, buying whatever is "in," or whatever you like. But you should consider your needs. Instead of following fashion, let fashion follow you. Identify your clothing personality so that you'll shop for what you really need.

First, determine what area of your life takes the greatest amount of your time. (*See* the wardrobe wheel on page 76).

I've listed four clothing personalities for you to study. Ascertain which image best describes you. Once you identify your own personality and your needs, you are on your way to becoming a wise dresser.

Type 1—Career Image

This is the woman who works in a formal atmosphere, usually behind a desk as an executive, manager, or administrator. She needs to keep the "office" image in mind. A conservative look is most often the answer. Elaborate, showy, and bold dressing would be out of place. A jacketed look is a must for the professional. Her wardrobe should include at least one quality suit, with immaculate detail in fit, fabric, line, and style. Jackets can coordinate with other skirts, dresses, and blouses. In a more casual atmosphere, jackets may be worn with well-fitted and tailored pants.

Type 2—Leisure Image

This woman spends her time as a homemaker, and is at her best in casual combinations. She is interested in comfort and practicality, not in the latest fashion look. Her main purchases will include a casual jacket and/or coat, jeans, and sturdy shoes or boots. At home, jeans and corduroy pants are suitable. A tweed jacket in a blazer style can pull the look together nicely for grocery shopping. A day or two each week she dons a lounge-hostess look.

For meetings and luncheons, skirts and jackets with silk-look blouses are ideal. Polyester means easy care, which is important to the homemaker. When going out in the evening, she will wear a two-piece silk-look dress of coordinated separates, and add accessories to make the look come alive.

Type 3—Evening Image

This woman may be a wife who joins her husband for entertaining in the evenings. She probably rarely deals with the public. Evening clothes in dressy combinations will be top priority in her closet. The major part of her budget is spent on evening clothes, with daytime rated second.

This woman can get a lot of use out of a simple dress with a flared skirt, and a silk top and pants in a fashion color and fabric. Accessories are a must and should be selected with extreme care. Glamour should be incorporated into her look. She'll go for glittery combs, small shoulder bags, bangles, and feathers for her hair. For her daytime look: pullover sweaters, wool skirts, corduroy pants, and a tweed jacket.

Type 4—Fashion Image

This woman works in a job which encourages creativity. She is not bound by dress codes. She is free to experiment with styles and trendy looks to express her own personality. She will regularly study fashion magazines and will, with excitement, try the "new" look. She'll wear the latest jackets and will try the newest look in pants and accessories.

What is your clothing image?

My clothing image is

Beautiful Color

. . . her own clothing is beautifully made—a purple gown of pure linen.

Proverbs 31:22

Beautiful Color

Color! It's all around you, that versatile and inexpensive accessory that adds real pizzazz to any fashion image. The most affordable of accents (it's free!), creative use of color proves invaluable in making the most of what you've got, and realizing your beauty potential.

You deal with color minute by minute from the time you are born. Though it sometimes assaults your senses, often you are unaware of the many ways that it affects you. Do you notice a difference in mood when you go from a pale yellow or white room to one done in dark wood and gray? Clichés such as "I'm green with envy," "I'm having a blue day," "I'm seeing red," and "I'm in the pink of things," prove that colors have become a great influence in everyday life.

Researchers have been fascinated by the power of color. Some of them claim that color is effective in fighting depression, calming aggression, increasing strength, aiding digestion, countering insomnia, and even in changing some personality traits.

Have you ever wondered why so many restaurants are decorated in red? Tests have shown that red makes people salivate. What better response could a restaurant owner hope for? Jail cell walls were painted pink after a study found that pink was effective in sapping anger, aggression, and physical strength.

Color also affects many of our value judgments. On first impression, a woman wearing a gray suit may be thought of as conservative and businesslike, while a woman wearing a bright red dress may be labeled exciting, stimulating, and romantic.

Most of us instinctively gravitate to certain colors. This color attraction has been explained by noted color analyst Johannes Itten. His theory originated in the 1800s, and holds that each individual possesses a natural color sense or instinct that selects his or her "subjective colors." These colors best express that person's personality, while enhancing and complementing hair, skin, and eye color as well.

You probably lean toward certain colors because they feel right and look good, too. It is very important to take advantage of the color group that does the most for you. Color groups are divided into two main categories: *warm* and *cool*. These divisions stem from the implications of the colors within them. The way we get our colors is to take the three primary colors of red, blue, and yellow. Red and blue with white and black added to produce shades and intensities, or red and blue together to create purple make the cool colors. Yellow alone or yellow added to any color is in the warm-color family.

Finding Your Best Colors

Warm colors include a myriad of shades of red, orange, and yellow.

Faces turn red when they are warm, the sun glows yellow to orange, strawberries ripen to red. Warm colors include a touch of yellow; cool colors do not.

Cool colors encompass the lavish hues of blues and greens. Cold oceans sparkle blue and green, green trees offer havens of shade, lips turn blue with cold. (*See* the samples for additional colors in the warm and cool families.)

The cool seasons are often described as summer and winter, and the warm seasons are spring and autumn. *These categories do not relate to seasonal dressing.*

To determine which season you are, study your hair, eye, and skin color. Try to base this as much as possible on your natural hair color and skin color (untanned). Use your natural eye color, without your tinted contacts. If you have difficulty determining your season, *put more emphasis on the skin tone,* as the skin is the background to which everything else relates.

There are several color-analysis programs available today, but after research and practical experience, I shall attempt to help you find your own colors through the theory which we have used for years at Image Improvement. If at all possible, try to find one of our Image Color Consultants, highly trained professionals who can help you understand and select your very best colors. If one is not available in your area, see the back of this book to order your fabric color swatches.

As you attempt to determine your best colors, remember that, generally speaking, the Cool Summer person has the all-American look—blond hair and blue eyes. The Cool Winter person has deeper, more intense coloring, with hair and eyes darker than the Cool Summer person.

The Warm Spring look includes strawberry blond to golden, bright red, and copper hair, with green to blue eyes. The Warm Autumn has deeper coloring in the eyes (usually in the brown tones) and hair than the Warm Spring person.

Colors have different meanings, and you should be aware of what certain colors suggest so that you can use color effectively with regard to your life-style and expectations.

Color Suggestions Worth

Remembering

1. Solid colors are best for suits, jackets, and dresses. Tweeds and muted plaids are also acceptable.

2. Navy and gray suits are great business colors for the executive.

3. White shirts, white blouses, and bright-colored blouses are very good for "authority" wear (worn *under* a jacket).

4. The more color contrast between blouse or shirt and suit, the more authoritative the look.

5. An all-black suit with white shirt or blouse can be so authoritative (especially on a tall woman) that it is often perceived as threatening.

6. Beige suits with blue shirts or blouses are excellent for the selling profession.

7. Polka dots, menswear stripes, some paisleys, and solid colors are excellent for ties and ascoted scarves.

8. A businesswoman may not be taken seriously when wearing a pink suit, which can suggest femininity or helplessness.

9. Yellow greens (olives) can subconsciously suggest suspicion about honesty and integrity. Avoid these colors, especially in the monies profession.

10. Purple, green, and gold are colors that are often offensive to others. Avoid them in large pieces of clothing such as suits, dresses, and jackets.

11. Brown suits and dresses test very well in the Midwest to western states. Avoid wearing them when dealing with someone from New York, Boston, and eastern states.

12. A beige, belted raincoat lends status.

13. Buy clothing only after you check the color in daylight. Store lighting often distorts the true color. You may be in for a surprise once you arrive home and check the color with your coordinates.

14. Don't throw away outfits that you discover are not your best colors. Place your best colors next to your face in your accessories. Buy new clothing only in your best colors and in time, your incorrect ones will be eliminated.

The above suggestions are primarily for the working woman (or man).

Cool Summer

Denise Nelson is a Cool Summer with pink undertones in her skin. She has ash tones in her hair and eyes that are gray toned.

Cool Summer

The Cool Summer person will usually have a fragile, soft appearance.

Skin: Very pink to pale beige, rose-toned beige, very light olive, or pink, with blue to rosy undertones.

Hair: Usually ash blond (a towhead), ash brown, taupe to dark brown, to gray. Cool Summers usually gray attractively. If your hair is blond, keep it blond or have it attractively frosted. If it is an ash tone, avoid red or warm-toned rinses. If you have dark brown hair, it is best to keep your natural hair color, or let it gray.

Eyes: Gray blues or gray greens, soft tones.

The colors for a Cool Summer are like a warm summer day in the shade. You look lovely in pastels, but some Cool Summer women can wear black. Your palette of colors will include:

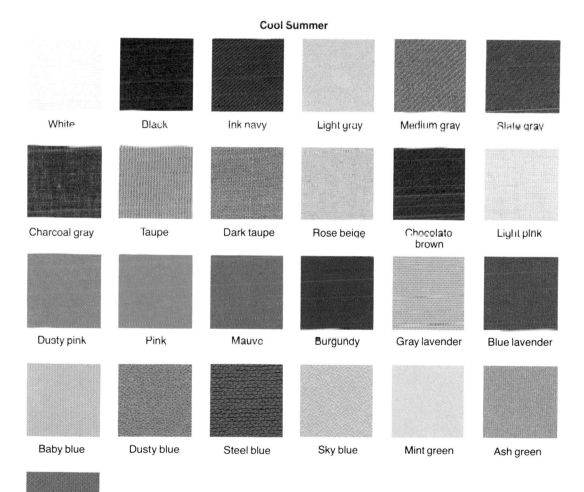

Cool Summer

White	Black	Ink navy	Light gray	Medium gray	Slate gray
Charcoal gray	Taupe	Dark taupe	Rose beige	Chocolate brown	Light pink
Dusty pink	Pink	Mauve	Burgundy	Gray lavender	Blue lavender
Baby blue	Dusty blue	Steel blue	Sky blue	Mint green	Ash green
Dusty green					

Actual colors may differ slightly.

Avoid such colors as orange, gold, yellow or yellow green, yellow brown, and rust.

Cool Winter

Jan Brehm is a Cool Winter with olive skin, dark brown hair, and blue eyes. Her hair and eye color are more intense and more contrasting than the Cool Summer.

Cool Winter

A Cool Winter person is known for her strong dramatic coloring. There is usually a definite dark-light contrast which is obvious in hair and skin.

Skin: Porcelain white skin, light to dark olive skin, pink or black brown skin. Some have deep rose beige skin colors. Most blacks and orientals also fall into this cool-season category.

Hair: God has blessed you with a beautiful asset—your hair coloring! It will usually be dark brown to black. Keep it in its natural color. If it grays (Winters often gray prematurely), it will be a lovely salt-and-pepper color. Frosting won't be flattering. Ash brown, blue black, and white hair colors are the Cool Winter types. As you grow older, your skin color will lighten, so allow your hair color to lighten, also. Keep your hair length short as the gray appears.

Eyes: Gray to dark blue, violet, dark brown, and gray green.

The colors for a Cool Winter are the elegant jewel tones. You look marvelous in black and contrasts. Your palette of colors will include:

Cool Winter

White	Black	Ink navy	Light gray	Medium gray	Slate gray
Charcoal gray	Taupe	Dark taupe	Rose beige	Chocolate brown	Pink
Hot pink	Strawberry rose	Blue red	Burgundy	Maroon	Mauve
Raspberry	Red violet	Purple	Sky blue	Steel blue	Sapphire blue
Royal blue	Blue teal	Green teal	Spruce green	Hunter green	

Actual colors may differ slightly.

Avoid these colors: gold, rust, yellow beige, or yellow green.

Warm Spring

Debi Wyant is a Warm Spring with skin color of golden undertones and golden brown freckles. Her hair has red highlights and her eyes have yellow highlights.

Warm Spring

A Warm Spring person has the coloring of a radiant spring day!

Skin: Ivory with peachy or golden undertones. Freckles may be obvious.

Hair: Will usually have warm brown to golden brown coloring. Strawberry blond, bright copper, golden gray, and flaxen or red brown hair coloring can be yours. Do not add ash color. If you gray, it's best to cover it all until you are completely gray, and then use a warm color. Do not frost your hair, but you may softly highlight it with a golden sun color.

Eyes: Hazel, topaz, golden brown and golden green, to blue green, blue, or turquoise.

The colors for a Warm Spring are clear and vivid. Yellow appears throughout your palette of color. Your colors will include:

Warm Spring

Ivory	Yellow beige	Camel	Peach camel	Golden camel	Warm brown
Cinnamon brown	Autumn brown	Royal navy	Yellow	Soft gold	Cantaloupe
Apricot	Peach	Salmon	Clear orange	Spring red	Rust
Spring blue	Medium turquoise	Apple green	Leaf green	Clear green	*Actual colors may differ slightly.*

Be certain to avoid such colors as black brown and all muted colors.

Warm Autumn

I am a Warm Autumn with warm golden tones in my skin. My eyes and hair are stronger in color intensity than the Warm Spring.

Warm Autumn

A Warm Autumn person will look marvelous in all the harvest-season colors.

Skin: Ivory, beige, gold, and copper skin. Peach, ivory, and freckles, too! Undertones are peachy.

Hair: Looks wonderful with red highlights. Redhead to auburn, brown with red or gold highlights, chestnut or yellow gray. Never use ash, and when you begin to gray, completely cover it with a warm color until you are all gray. Avoid frosting your hair, but highlights can add warmth.

Eyes: Golden to dark brown, amber to hazel, golden green to green and aqua turquoise.

A Warm Autumn looks smashing in colorful, intense, tangy, spicy, earthy colors. All your reds have yellow in them. Your palette of colors will include:

Warm Autumn

Ivory	Yellow beige	Camel	Peach camel	Golden camel	Warm brown
Cinnamon brown	Autumn brown	Royal navy	Soft gold	Sun yellow	Gold
Yellow gold	Clear green	Kelly green	Warm forest green	Avocado	Moss green
Medium turquoise	Turquoise	Peach	Salmon	Apricot	Coral
Clear orange	Tangerine	Spring red	Orange red	Rust	Deep rust

Avoid such colors as gray, purple, pink, and burgundy. Actual colors may differ slightly.

Colors for Wardrobe Coordination

To work toward a color-coordinated wardrobe, study chapters 6 and 8, and then select three colors which you feel will work together for your wardrobe combinations. These three colors should be a basic, a neutral, and a color for workability. Use these colors for the pieces of clothing which are largest in size, such as skirts, pants, suits, and dresses. The rest of the colors on your palette can be used in blouses and smaller items of clothing. To begin your planning, fill out the lines below. I have also provided a *sample* idea for you regarding each season of color. The choice is up to you.

Cool Summer

_____

_____

_____

(Example: ink navy, plum, pale taupe.)

Cool Winter

_____

_____

_____

(Example: black, gray, berry, or red; white for summer months.)

Warm Spring

_____

_____

_____

(Example: honey beige, coral, ivory. Royal navy blue is great year-round.)

Warm Autumn

_____

_____

_____

(Example: warm brown, russet, camel. Ivory is lovely on you.)

With your colors in mind, carefully study chapter 17 on makeup and skin care.

When you use your very best colors, neutrals and basics, you are in harmony with your natural color palette, and you will look your best. The world of color is exciting, and the combinations and possibilities are only as limited as your imagination!

Closet Checklist

Now that you know your season type and your color palette, check your closet to see how many of the correct colors are included in the clothes you now own.

Cool Summer

White	_____	Pink	_____
Black	_____	Mauve	_____
Ink navy	_____	Burgundy	_____
Light gray	_____	Gray lavender	_____
Medium gray	_____	Blue lavender	_____
Slate gray	_____	Baby blue	_____
Charcoal gray	_____	Dusty blue	_____
Taupe	_____	Steel blue	_____
Dark taupe	_____	Sky blue	_____
Rose beige	_____	Mint green	_____
Chocolate brown	_____	Ash green	_____
Light pink	_____	Dusty green	_____
Dusty pink	_____		

Cool Winter

White	_____	Burgundy	_____
Black	_____	Maroon	_____
Ink navy	_____	Mauve	_____
Light gray	_____	Raspberry	_____
Medium gray	_____	Red violet	_____
Slate gray	_____	Purple	_____
Charcoal gray	_____	Sky blue	_____
Taupe	_____	Steel blue	_____
Dark taupe	_____	Sapphire blue	_____
Rose beige	_____	Royal blue	_____
Chocolate brown	_____	Blue teal	_____
Pink	_____	Green teal	_____
Hot pink	_____	Spruce green	_____
Strawberry rose	_____	Hunter green	_____
Blue red	_____		

Warm Spring

Ivory	_____	Apricot	_____
Yellow beige	_____	Peach	_____
Camel	_____	Salmon	_____
Peach camel	_____	Clear orange	_____
Golden camel	_____	Spring red	_____
Warm brown	_____	Rust	_____
Cinnamon brown	_____	Spring blue	_____
Autumn brown	_____	Medium turquoise	_____
Royal navy	_____	Apple green	_____
Yellow	_____	Leaf green	_____
Soft gold	_____	Clear green	_____
Cantaloupe	_____		

Warm Autumn

Ivory	_____	Warm forest green	_____
Yellow beige	_____	Avocado	_____
Camel	_____	Moss green	_____
Peach camel	_____	Medium turquoise	_____
Golden camel	_____	Turquoise	_____
Warm brown	_____	Peach	_____
Cinnamon brown	_____	Salmon	_____
Autumn brown	_____	Apricot	_____
Royal navy	_____	Coral	_____
Soft gold	_____	Clear orange	_____
Sun yellow	_____	Tangerine	_____
Gold	_____	Spring red	_____
Yellow gold	_____	Orange red	_____
Clear green	_____	Rust	_____
Kelly green	_____	Deep rust	_____

Nobody Is Perfect

A wise woman builds her house, while a foolish woman tears hers down by her own efforts.

Proverbs 14:1

Nobody is perfect. Unfortunately, this is a fact. You may never have "ideal" measurements or a flawless face. Don't despair! You can still *look* as though you do!

The trick is to learn which clothes will enhance your best features and help hide your faults at the same time! In other words, make the most of what you've got!

Emily Cho, coauthor of *Looking Terrific,* warns, however:

> Be careful that your clothing does not become a series of masks for various parts of your body. Sometimes I see a woman who has so thoroughly mastered the methods of camouflaging her body's problems that she's totally dull. She's the one you *always* see in a navy gabardine pantsuit with too long a jacket. Her figure solution is so successful that nobody looks at her. They might not know she has big hips, but who cares? They don't know that she has personality either for that, too, is hidden.

Be balance conscious, bear in mind your own unique personality as created in the image of God, remember the tips I am giving you, and you can't go wrong.

First things first. Are you large or small boned? Are you long or short waisted? The ideal figure is proportioned with half the length of her body above the hip and half below. The lower half will be evenly divided by the knees. The shoulders should measure the same distance in inches as the measurement from the nape of the neck to the waist back. The ideal figure fits into a T for the top of the body. Ideally, the bust and hip measurements should be the same, the waist 10 inches smaller (36-26-36).

A great many American women are short waisted, and a great many have heavy upper thighs. They also have hips one skirt size larger and two pants sizes larger than their blouse size. Some women have well-rounded torsos, others are wide and flat. Few figures are ideal. Let's work with your body and make it look its absolute best.

Now fill out the rest of your measurements and compare them with the American standard measurement chart on page 49.

Measuring Chart

Measure without shoes on, standing tall and straight.

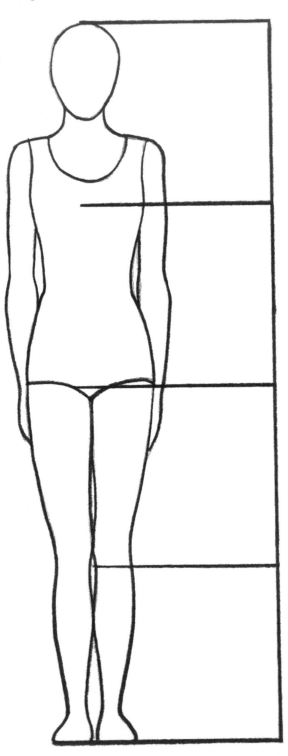

Measurement from top of hairline to fullest
  point of bust line _____
Measurement from bust line to hips _____
Measurement from hips to knees _____
Measurement from knees to floor _____

Height   _____
Bust   _____
Hip   _____
Wrist   _____
Weight   _____
Waist   _____
Thigh   _____
Bone structure _____

My figure problems are (mark areas that
apply to you):

Height-Weight

Tall, thin   _____
Tall, medium   _____
Tall, large   _____
Average, thin   _____
Average, medium   _____
Average, large   _____
Short, thin   _____
Short, average   _____
Short, large   _____
Short waisted   _____
Long waisted   _____
Long legged   _____
Short legged   _____

Body Type

Neck too long   _____
Neck too short   _____
Double chin   _____
Shoulders too broad _____
Shoulders too narrow _____
Bust too large   _____
Bust too small   _____
Waist too large   _____
Waist too small   _____
Abdomen too large   _____
Arms too thin   _____
Arms too large   _____
Hips too small   _____
Hips too large   _____
Legs too large   _____

Areas to dress carefully are

_____

_____   _____

_____

A dressmaker gave me a chart of the typical proportions of most American women.
See how closely you fit into the "mold."

Typical American Standard Body Proportions

Dress Size	Bust	Waist	Hips
6	33"	24½"	36"
8	34"	26"	37"
10	35"–36"	27½"	38"
12	36"	29"	39"
14	38"	30½"	40"
16	40"	32"	41"
18	42"	33½"	42"

Use line, style, pattern, and color to avoid
accentuating not-perfect features. Create
visual illusion with your wardrobe to make
yourself appear proportionately balanced.
Let's go on to see just how to do that.

Visual Illusions Through Line

Many of us don't realize the importance of
"line" in dressing. Line can make you look
taller and slimmer, or shorter and heavier.
Visual illusion is the key to line dressing. In
the example below, both lines are exactly the
same length; but notice how much shorter
the top line appears. This is a visual illusion.

Consider these illusions when planning your best clothing selections.

(1) The vertical line is very slimming. For this look, avoid anything that will prevent the eye from moving up the figure.

(2) This line will add height and is often called the "magic Y." Very good for a slenderizing effect.

(3) Two vertical lines placed close together can give a slimming and lengthening look.

(4) Two vertical lines placed far apart will definitely add weight and shorten a figure. They form three wide panels that draw the eye *across* the body.

(5) This line will definitely accentuate the bust line, and the longer the eye moves upward without a horizontal line, the taller the figure will appear.

(6) The sooner the eye meets a horizontal line, the shorter the figure will appear.

(7) This line will add width at the waist and will make the figure appear shorter.

(8) This line accentuates the bust line and gives the appearance of shortness and width.

(9) Princess line. A young line that is almost never flattering to a mature figure. The two opposing lines will make a figure appear shorter, accentuate the weight at the bust line, the hips, and the midriff, and also will emphasize bony hips.

(10) Asymmetrical line which can disguise figure imbalances, plus add interest and sophistication.

(11) Diagonal line creates interest, but will make you appear slightly shorter and thinner. Good for most figures except overly tall and slim, or short and thin.

5'8" and Taller

(Average Weight)

If you are tall, you should wear clothes that move with your body, a contrast of soft silhouettes, unfussy looks. A tall woman with a good figure can look striking in a large-print fabric if the gown is floor-length.

The taller-than-average type

Dressing Dos

Do wear
dressmaker suits and dresses with soft lines
styles with long jackets, low waistlines
three-quarter-length jackets
single- and double-breasted jackets
hipline (and longer) jackets
two-piece dresses
straight, flared, or pleated skirts
outfits in contrasting colors; bright-color contrasts
bold-patterned fabrics
textured fabrics
horizontal lines
lines that cut below the waist
large-scale accessories
wide collars
wide belts in bold colors
moderate heels (not flats)

Wear clothes that focus on simplicity without severity. Maintain your femininity.

Dressing Don'ts

Don't wear
clothes that cover your whole body; let some of your skin show
tight or clinging fabrics without a contrasting softness
your skirts or your hair too short
short-waisted dresses
boleros
severely tailored, slim, or skimpy clothing
a shift that has no horizontal lines
large vertical stripes

5'2" and Shorter,

and Petite

Don't think "short"! Give an illusion of tall-ness. A lot of your success depends on the way you project yourself. Any garment too complicated, too big, or too bulky will over-power you. As long as the proportions fit your figure, most silhouettes will work. Be careful to dress as though *you* are wearing the *clothes*—not the other way around!

The shorter-than-average type

Dressing Dos

Do wear
smooth and slim one-piece dresses
either pencil-slim skirts or slightly flared
   ones
fitted coats and suit jackets
a short spencer jacket—this gives a leggier
   appearance
short hipbone and waist-length jackets, and
   boleros
jump suits that don't nip in at the waist
classic trousers with high heels
one color, or a soft mix of colors
light colors, if you are also thin
clothes that create a proportioned look
vertical lines and small patterns
dainty florals, stars, and dots to suggest femininity, softness, and youth
high waistlines or princess styles
smooth fabrics
narrow belts, same color as dress
broad white collars, pointed collars, or V
   necklines
a line of vertical buttons
bright scarves
classic pearls and thin chains
soft, lace-collared blouses
pumps

Dressing Don'ts

Don't wear
skirts that are either too long or too short—
   short-short skirts will make you look even
   shorter
contrasting bold colors

large, overly brilliant floral designs
big-brimmed hats, six-foot mufflers, and so
　　on
extreme hats or hairstyles
jewelry that clutters and shortens your neck
large pockets or oversized lapels
cuffs on pants
extremely high heels (over three inches)—
　　they will look too arched and obvious
clunky shoes, or ankle or T straps
patterned stockings

5′5″ to 5′6″ and Average

Consider yourself lucky if you are average. A lot can be said for Ms. In-Between. What may look overpowering on the small girl, or too insignificant on the tall girl, probably will be just fine for you. You can get away with frills and high heels, prints and stripes (either vertical or horizontal). Shopping is fun for you. You seldom have to ask for alterations.

Color, used tastefully, can be all the "lift" you need. Jewelry should be average size. Just don't let your averageness be boring. Use your imagination . . . make fashion fun!

The average type

Too Thin

(Average Height or Taller)

A thin woman can wear anything and never look heavy, but you can look too thin if you wear something very bare or clingy. Soft fullness is best, and you should cover any part of your body that looks skinny in proportion to the rest.

The very thin type

Dressing Dos

Do wear
gentle, soft lines
blouson dresses and blouses
shirtwaist dresses with long, full sleeves
dresses with full-cut bodices that nip in at the
    waist and flare out over hips
gathered skirts
pantsuits
the layered fashion
fabrics which are soft and full, giving the il-
    lusion of more shape
light colors, plaids, checks, and patterns
contrasting colors
waistlines made with colored separates and
    belts
soft cowl necklines
soft, puffy, rounded accessories
textured stockings
light or bright tights
scarves at the neckline
chokers and dickeys
boots under a skirt to camouflage thin legs

Walk tall and straight!

Dressing Don'ts

Don't wear
anything bare or clingy, short or skimpy
clothes that are too long
straight-line coats
pencil-slim skirts
tubular dresses
dark, one-color garments

vertical lines
large prints
clothes that create a severe look
scoop or wide-open necklines
off-shoulder, halter, or V-neckline styles
prissy bows and ruffles
heavy shoes

Don't wear halter necks if you're flat chested, or bare shoulders if you're bone thin. Keep everything covered. Remember that shorts look better than Bermudas.

The Large-Framed, Full-Figured Woman

The large, full-figured woman's clothing must fit perfectly, especially through the shoulders. A big, loose tent never helps. Try a touch of color at the face, keeping the attention upward. All attention should be focused on your face, away from your body.

Dressing Dos

Do wear
jackets without lapels
skirts that have a slight flare
V-neck cardigans
solid-color fabrics or *small* prints
medium to lightweight fabrics that have a dull
    finish
vertical lines
contrasting-colored buttons—these are slim-
    ming if they are located down the center of
    a coat or dress
diagonal lines at the bust line
darker colors in an unbroken line
full- or three-quarter-length sleeves
V necklines and long necklaces
narrow self-belts, or none at all
brimmed hats; pillboxes make one look
    larger
simple shoes—pumps or slingbacks

The look-too-heavy figure

Dressing Don'ts

Don't wear
front-pleated or dirndl skirts—extra fabric adds pounds
loose tent shapes
tight clothing, or too-large clothing
shiny fabrics such as satin
heavy and bulky wools
stiff fabrics
clingy fabrics such as jersey
horizontal lines
a large expanse of bold pattern

plaids and two-color outfits—stripes add pounds
oversized collars, cuffs, and shoulders
square or sweetheart necks
sleeveless or strapless styles

Don't be tempted by the appeal of some prints. Remember, they may look better on a wall than on a body!

What to Wear From Head to Toe

Pointed Chin

Double Chin

Receding Chin

Lines in Neck

If you have a *pointed chin* wear wide, square necklines, or wide, round necklines; choose soft patterns

If you have a *slightly receding chin* wear low necklines and rolled collars to accentuate shoulders

If you have a *double chin* wear plain necklines and long beads; center all attention on hair and eyes

If you have *lines* in your *neck* wear beautiful scarves or high-necked collars

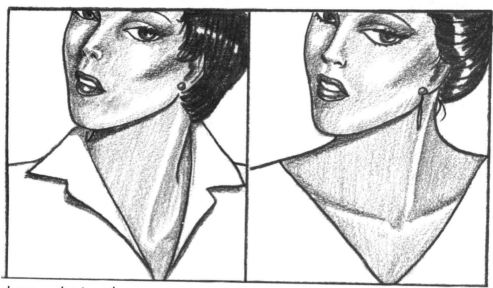

If you have a *short neck* wear
V or open necklines
pointed Revere collars
long necklaces and pendants
lighter colors at the neck, with contrasting
   accents
swept-up hat brims or brimless hats
short hairstyles that sweep up

Don't wear
round, high, or square necklines
Peter Pan collars, high or rolled collars
bows or scarves under the chin
choker beads
long hair

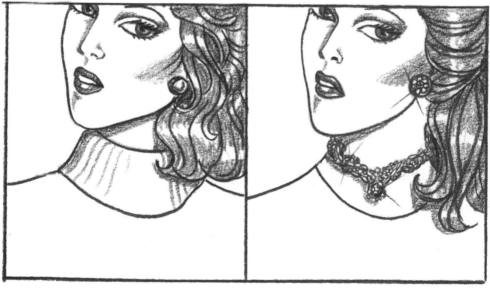

If you have a *long neck* wear
high necklines filled in with scarves, chokers,
   and dog collars
Peter Pans and jewel necklines
round earrings
hair styled low on the neck
hats with a downward line

Don't wear
V necks, plunging or low necklines
long pendants or long earrings
oval necklines or strapless styles
short, short hair

If you have *narrow, sloping shoulders* wear
V necklines
double-breasted jackets
straight-fitting vests, boleros, and boxy
    jackets
slightly tucked or gathered styles
wide lapels, puffed sleeves, and short capes
shoulder pads
horizontal yokes and lines

Don't wear
tight-fitting waists or jackets
diagonal lines that accent the slope
raglan, dolman, or kimono sleeves
long, tight sleeves or armseye
halters or fussy necklines with lots of lace or
    bows
unpadded shoulders

If you have *square shoulders* wear
raglan sleeves

Don't wear
horizontal patterns or bateau necklines

If you have *broad, wide shoulders* wear
unconstructed shirts and jackets with easy
    shoulder lines
shoulder lines one inch inside your natural
    shoulder line
dropped shoulders, raglan, and shoulders
    without a defined line
narrow lapels and halter necklines
vests and lower necklines
diagonal interest at pocket hipline

Don't wear
puckered shoulder lines, shoulder pads or
    shoulder trim, accent or color
high necklines or unbroken width
horizontal lines at the waist

If you have *round shoulders* wear
slightly bloused bodices
collars that stand away from the neck
set-in sleeves

Don't wear
princess styles or drop shoulders

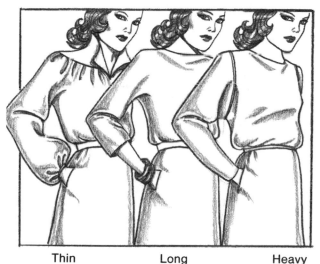

Thin   Long   Heavy

If you have *thin arms* wear
sleeves that fit loosely
sleeves wider and fuller above the elbow
draped, bulky sleeves, fitted at the wrist
elbow- or bracelet-length sleeves with wide-
    trimmed cuffs

Don't wear
sleeveless garments or cap sleeves
strapless gowns
tight-fitting sleeves (unless they are of bulky,
    textured fabrics)

If you have *long arms* wear
three-quarter-length sleeves with contrast-
    ing gloves
large bracelets

If you have *heavy arms* wear
raglan, kimono, or dolman sleeves
either very long or very short sleeves
long, unbroken sleeve line, without cuffs
wide armhole cuts

Don't wear
tight sleeves
sleeveless, off-shoulder, or strapless styles
    (use a stole)
cuffs or puffed sleeves
snug or sweater knits

Flabby or heavy arms in a sleeveless dress
will age you and give you a slightly frumpy
air, even if everything else is perfect.

If you have a *small bust* wear
a bra with excellent support, underwired and
   with comfortable straps
blouson tops that drop softly below the
   waistline
sweat-shirt-style tops in silks
longer, slightly flared A-line or straight skirts

If you have a *large bust* wear
dark colors on top, lighter on the bottom
diagonal lines
V necks
raglan or dolman sleeves with some fullness

Don't wear
fitted jackets or coats
double-breasted jackets
cowl-necked sweaters
clinging tops
shiny or heavy fabrics
tight-fitting or empire waists
square or round necklines
horizontal lines at yoke or waist
tight-fitting or puffed sleeves

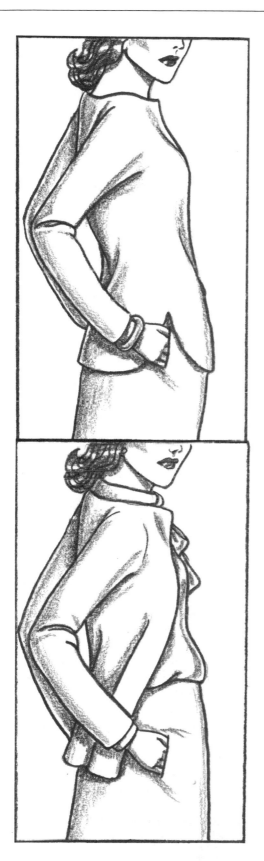

If you have a *swayback* wear
overblouses with unfitted waistlines; practice
  correct posture

If you have a *thick waist* wear
chemise, drop waists, and long lines
Chanel-type jackets
dresses with bloused backs
loose sheaths and blouson waists that drop
  somewhat; clothes that fit loosely
a narrow belt the same color as the outfit, if a
  belt must be worn
belts that drape around the hip area
an underall sheer Lycra body stocking to
  give a smooth line

Don't wear
princess or A-line styles
most belts, including cinch, cummerbunds,
  or anything that dramatically calls attention to your middle

If you have a *short waist* wear
blouson tops
tops outside
tunic tops
ruffled-neck blouses or loosely wrapped and
    knotted scarves
longer sweaters with long pants or slim skirts
loose layers
outfits of one color or close-tone colors
narrow waistbands that sit below the waist

Don't wear
waist-defining separates
high trouser waistbands
two colors that meet at the waist; horizontal
    lines at the waist
wide belts

If you have a *protruding abdomen* wear
tunics and chemises that hang softly over the
    abdomen
waistless dresses and overblouses
loosely belted jump suits without too much
    bulk or body
A-line skirts
skirts with pleats sewn down to about four
    and one-half inches—these have a gir-
    dling effect
trousers with soft pleats at the waistline
hard-finish fabrics
tiny florals over the protruding area—these
    may be more slimming than solid colors in
    some fabrics
side drapes
side-slash pockets to divert the eye

Don't wear
straight, bouffant, or gored skirts
clingy fabrics or fabrics that hang heavily
    over the stomach
cotton jersey or ribbed knits
tight belts

If you have a *flat derriere* wear
two-piece rather than one-piece knits
gathered skirts, fullness

If you have a *large derriere* wear
things that float from the shoulders and arms,
   such as caftans and chemises; long vests
   are great
layering over pants (Pants must fit to perfec-
   tion!)
dirndls and softly pleated skirts

Don't wear
pants that are too tight or skirts that cling
knits that bind and stretch around your derriere
shirts that tuck in tightly at the waist without a
   cover-up
short vests

If you have *large hips* wear
vertical lines that draw the eye up and down
over-the-hip-length jackets with pants (Pants
   should fit perfectly.)
slightly flared skirts
box jackets with skirts
pants with jackets unbuttoned
dark skirts with lighter tops
duller fabrics
styles with a broader shoulder line

Don't wear
slim skirts, pleats, gathers, or extra fullness
skirts cut on the bias
pleated-front pants or skirts
fitted jackets
below-waistline trimming, detail, or attention
plaids and horizontal stripes
bold print skirts or fabrics of shiny or flimsy
   texture
two-color contrasting lines at the hip area
pocket detail

Don't emphasize your waist, even if it is
proportionately smaller, as this will "hourglass" your figure.

If you have unattractive legs (thick ankles, heavy calves, bulging thighs), a tailored jump suit with a straight trouser leg (or one slightly tapered at the ankle) is an excellent way to cover up the problem. Pants, of course, are another camouflaging alternative. For heavy thighs or calves, select pants with a fuller cut, in a nonclinging fabric—twill, gabardine, cotton poplin. In general, knits are not for you. Neither are knickers, jodhpurs, or the new knee shorts.

You Can Wear Pants!

In recent years, the fashion focus has often been on pants. Many women have dreaded this because they felt they couldn't wear pants. Well, no more! Almost anyone can wear pants.

The following pictures illustrate different figure types and the pants sets that look best on these types. Study the drawings and let these solutions work for you.

(1) This figure is usually a size smaller on top than on the bottom. Camouflage large hips by wearing simple tailored pants exclusive of ornamentation, such as tabs or pocket flaps. Jackets need to be long enough to cover the hips, and the blouses should have a softening effect. A bowed blouse is ideal (this also draws attention to the face, not the hips!).

(2) This figure is hippy but small waisted—an hourglass shape. Menswear construction in pants allows the flexibility needed. You can easily take in or let out the waistline. To emphasize a small waist and minimize hips, wear an interesting belt and a jacket that just reaches below the hip.

(3) This is the well-proportioned, tall, slender figure that most women envy! Pants of all types look great on this figure. Experiment with different styles: try pleated trousers, short jacket, and a dressy blouse. Use your imagination!

(4) The short, stocky figure needs a slimming and elongating illusion. This can be achieved by wearing pants and jackets in matching colors. Try pants with a crisply pressed pleat. To conceal a waist problem, try a sweater vest.

(5) Legs, legs, legs, and a short waist. Is this your problem? To help lengthen your torso, try a blouson top pulled below the waistline, and elastic-waist pants. "Low rise" pants that sit on the hips can also help.

(6) A tall, large-boned (but not heavy) figure can handle plaid pants. To complete the look, wear them with a solid-color jacket and a bulky sweater to offset the pattern of the pants.

(7) The slightly overweight figure with a thick waistline. Try this classic but eye-catching look. The dark, solid-color pants are slimming and combined with the long, V-neck vest, your waistline can be minimized. The cape covers the hip area and completes the look.

(8) This figure is large boned and short waisted. To look great in pants, wear pants with a contour waistband. Solid colors in matching pantsuits work best, as they give you a put-together look that draws attention away from the waistline. Keeping the jacket buttoned also aids this illusion.

(9) The slim-hipped, long-legged figure. The person with this type of figure often has a difficult time finding pants that are long enough. If so, why not try Bermuda shorts? If that isn't your style, try tailored, slim-fitting pants such as designers make. To add fullness at the hips, try pants that are pleated at the waistline.

(10) The short, curvy figure. Often this type of woman wants to look taller. Make sure your clothes are the perfect proportion. Try hem lengths that fall just to the back of your shoe, and use vertical stripes for added leg lengthening. You can also try "high rise" pants that have a deep waistband and hit the waist higher than usual—this draws the eye upward and lengthens the leg.

(11) Petite, boyish figure. This type requires simplicity yet sophistication. Try classic trousers and blazers. Proportion is essential. If you look for the new lines in petite sizes, you can find pants you won't have to shorten.

If you still are saying no to pants, try this: For evening, wear a 360-degree skirt that stops just at the ankle (only if you are tall). For daytime, aim for tonality. This means matching the color tones of a skirt, stocking, and shoe: gray suit, sheer gray hose, slightly deeper gray shoe. Don't wear shoes with ankle straps. Keep hemlines at the knee or a little longer.

The Inside Story

In the end, people appreciate frankness more than flattery.

Proverbs 28:23

One of the most essential beauty aids, and one we often neglect, is the right undergarments.

You can subtract ten years in ten minutes and look ten pounds thinner by using the correct underwear. This simply means knowing all the techniques of fitting and how to choose the correct underwear for you and your shape.

What's the inside story? The right bra. How to find the proper size? Easy math! A tape measure and you.

First, measure around the chest area at the rib cage, directly under the breast. (*See* Diagram 1.) Do this without a bra on. Pull the tape measure snug. Whatever the measurement, just add five inches to it and that's your bra size. Example: If you measure an underbust of thirty inches, add five for a total of thirty-five inches. If your underbust measurement is twenty-eight inches, add five for a total of thirty-three. If it is the odd number, take both the smaller and larger size bras from several different manufacturers, and decide in the fitting room which size fits you best.

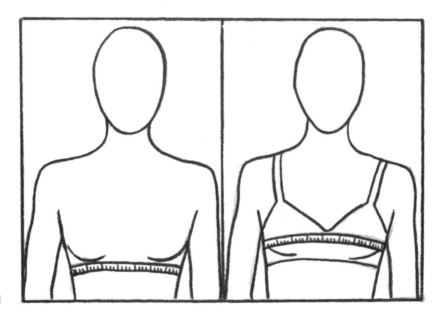

Diagram 1   Diagram 2

To find your cup size, put your bra on, centering the cup. (*See* Diagram 2.) Pull the tape measure around you again, and measure yourself at the fullest point. If that number is one inch larger than your underbust measurement, you wear an A cup bra; two inches larger, you wear a B cup; three inches larger, you wear a C cup; and four inches larger, a D cup.

Now, are you wearing the wrong type of bra?

Here's how to find the right one. Straps should be tight, but not pinch the skin. Straps should keep cups smooth, not provide support and uplift—the cups are supposed to do that. Cups should be filled out all the way to the tip. Check to see if the bra fits close to the body and clings to the breastbone. There should be no flesh bulge above the bra in front, back, or on the sides.

Bras must fit correctly, and they should be tried on just the same as a dress or suit.

Select a color for all your undergarments that is close to your skin color. Beige is much better to wear under white or light clothing than white. White shows through white pants, blouses, and sweater knits. Beige or skin color does not. Of course, avoid polka dots and stripes.

Did you ever see a woman in white casual pants bend over to pick up a box of laundry detergent in the grocery store, and you could see the obvious line of her yellow bikini polka-dot panties? '

When trying on a bra, dress for the occasion. Wear a clinging sweater or silk blouse and you will see immediately whether or not the new bra will look well under smooth fabrics.

Avoid lacy or highly decorative bras and underclothes, as they may give you an uneven look. Bras, panties, and slips should be invisible.

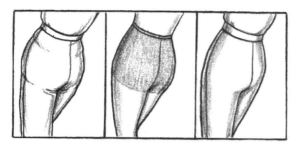

With pants, wear control-top panty hose with invisible lines, or a lightweight spandex brief that extends from hip to waist. Even if you are a size 8, never wear bikini underpants under light-colored or tight slacks.

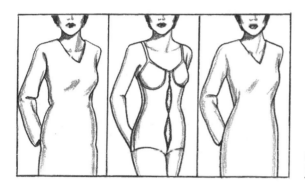

An all-in-one paneled body shaper can be a marvelous camouflage under a revealing jersey dress.

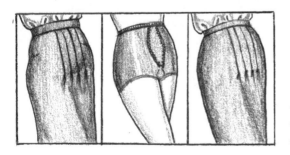

A special stomach-slimming panel in control-top panty hose can be just the thing to wear under a sewn-down pleated skirt that doesn't cover up a tummy bulge.

Planning Your Wardrobe

Any enterprise is built by wise planning, becomes strong through common sense, and profits wonderfully by keeping abreast of the facts.

Proverbs 24:3, 4

My daughter, Deanna, attended a private Christian high school that enforced a dress code. The girls were required to wear skirts, blouses, jackets, or dresses to school every day.

Deanna has a cousin, Sue, who attended a public school that had no dress code. When those two girls got together to shop, they ended up going in opposite directions! Sue shopped for pants or jeans, while Deanna selected dresses.

Now, you wouldn't say either girl was wrong in making her clothing choices. They just had different clothing needs.

The Wardrobe Wheel

When you plan your wardrobe, think in terms of clothing that will be worn every day. If you select items with care, they will last a long time, look good, and supply you with a closetful of confidence.

If you are like most women, you probably have a closetful of clothes you can't or don't wear. Most of the items do not coordinate with more than what came with the original purchase. It's easy to be an impulse buyer, but very dangerous to your pocketbook, because you will not get the results in wardrobe coordination that you need.

To find out how much time you spend on different activities during your waking hours, think in terms of a "wardrobe wheel."

This idea, which I originally saw in *Glamour* magazine, is invaluable for budgeting wardrobe expenses. The largest wedge of the wardrobe wheel will indicate your greatest wardrobe needs, and you can then shop accordingly.

The example shows a working woman's wheel. Study this example and then fill out your own activity time chart. (You might want to fill it out in pencil, as your life-style may change over the months and years.) The chart is based on one week with 112 waking hours.

5 Hrs. Continuing Education

7 Hrs. Private Time

6 Hrs. Sports, Hobby

4 Hrs. Church

10 Hrs. Family Recreation

30 Hrs. Housework Cooking Child Care

50 Hrs. Work (including dressing and driving time)

See run jump

How to Budget

To determine your activity time for the average week, fill out the following:

Activity	Weekly Hours
Work (outside the home, or in a home office)	_____
Housework, shopping, cooking, child care	_____
Private meditation time	_____
Church and related activities	_____
Club and community activities	_____
Theater, dining, entertaining	_____
Special classes, hobbies, sports	_____
Family recreation	_____

This chart allows for 16 waking hours and 8 hours of sleep in each 24-hour period. The total weekly waking hours is 112.

Chart your activity time here on your wardrobe wheel.

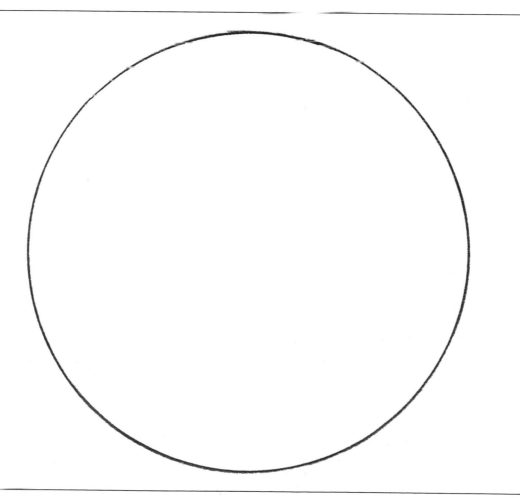

Building a Wardrobe

Creating a wardrobe that enhances and brings out the best "you" is not at all impossible. Listed below are a few steps that can produce rewarding results.

Begin by treating yourself to a couple of quiet hours alone with a cup of coffee, paper, and pencil. Now, let's begin.

Ask yourself the following questions, and write down the answers.

What type of inner person are you (dramatic, efficient, quiet, cheerful)? Choose two adjectives to describe yourself.

1. _____

2. _____

Mark the space that best describes your clothing style.

_____ *Classic conservative clothing* the skirted suit, shirtwaist dress. (For office worker, banker, insurance agent, real estate agent, business executive, manager.)

_____ *Classic sporty clothing* tweed or corduroy blazer, plaid shirt, synthetic-blend pants, or washable skirts. (For teacher, social coordinator, school counselor, youth worker, sports director.)

_____ *High-fashion, trendy clothing* new fashion looks and up-to-the-minute clothing. (For fashion salesperson, beautician, professional fashion model, entertainer, hostess, and travel agent.)

_____ *Casual clothing* pants and turtleneck, jeans and shirt. (For factory worker, production worker, maintenance person, construction worker, housekeeper.)

What are the assets and liabilities in your figure? Large waist, small bust? Don't worry about how many liabilities you have because there is a solution for each one. (*See* chapter 4 to understand your figure.)

Assets

_____

_____

_____

Liabilities

_____

_____

_____

Which of your best colors have you chosen for your major "investment" clothing coordination? (*See* chapter 3 to refresh your memory.) Select only two or three interchangeable colors for your basic clothing pieces.

1. _____

2. _____

3. _____

Define the particular clothing needs for your life-style. Use the activity chart on page 77. What type of clothing, and how much of each kind, do you need?

_____

_____

_____

After you decide on the style (chapter 2) and color (chapter 3) that is best for you, and have "uncluttered" your closet (chapter 7), list all the clothing that you are *presently* wearing, describing type and color.

Jackets/Suits

_____   _____

_____   _____

Skirts

_____   _____

_____   _____

Blouses/Shirts/Tops

_____   _____

_____   _____

_____   _____

Dresses

_____   _____

_____   _____

_____   _____

Pants

_____   _____

_____   _____

Sweaters

_____   _____

_____   _____

Miscellaneous

_____   _____

_____   _____

Following is a list of the basic items needed to start building a versatile wardrobe. The fabrics and styles will differ with summer and winter clothing. In warmer climates, summer clothing will be worn for most of the year. In cooler climates, winter clothing will be worn for longer periods of time. Adjust your selections to the climate, making sure certain garments have long wearing potential. On the right, check the clothing you now have that is color coordinated for you.

Basic Versatile Wardrobe	*Your Pieces* (√)
1 3-piece suit (jacket, skirt, pants)	_____
1 blazer or jacket	_____
2 basic skirts	_____
1 classic pair of pants	_____
3 to 6 blouses or shirts	_____
1 tunic-type top	_____
2 versatile basic or shirt dresses	_____
1 cardigan sweater	_____
1 pair of jeans	_____
1 hostess caftan gown	_____
1 year-round trench coat (removable lining)	_____
2 pairs of shoes (1 pump and 1 sandal) and accessories to match	_____

Keep all of the above items in two or three solid colors that color coordinate. For interest, add a couple of blouses in a soft check or plaid, but to have a workable wardrobe you must use solid colors for your core items.

This list is the backbone of a good wardrobe. The working woman will expand with more skirts and jackets, the homemaker with more casual clothing, and the student with sports-type selections.

List additional pieces (in order of importance) that you need to complete your wardrobe.

_____

_____

_____

_____

_____

_____

_____

_____

To work these items into your budget, decide what you will purchase (or make) over the next three to six months. (Limit yourself to no more than three major items each month.)

First month: _____

_____

Second month: _____

_____

Third month: _____

_____

Fourth month: _____

_____

_____

What Is Investment Dressing?

Have you ever had a jacket or favorite suit that you just can't seem to wear out—you've had it for years and it still looks new? That's what investment dressing is all about. It's clothing that lasts, can be worn year after year, has a classic style, and is made from quality fabric.

With clothing prices skyrocketing, investment dressing is more important than ever. Start thinking in terms of cost for each wearing. An inexpensive skirt may seem like a good buy, but if you wear it only ten times, the cost is too high. On the other hand, if you get a good-quality wool suit and wear it two times a week for four years (456 wearings!)

that's investment dressing, and the cost for each wearing is a bargain!

You'll find a sample chart below. The next time you shop for an article of clothing, consider what it costs and how long it will be worn.

For investment dressing, follow these simple rules:

1. Purchase a garment of the best fabric, workmanship, and quality that you can afford.
2. Select neutrals and basic colors for optimum year-round wear (beige, gray, navy, black, brown, and white). They work best for coordinating outfits. Chapter 3 on color helped you find your best colors.
3. Choose accessories in bright colors and ones that are "fun" items.
4. What are your wardrobe needs? What clothes do you need for your life-style? (Remember your wardrobe wheel on page 76.)
5. Select clothing that can do double or triple duty for those day-into-evening occasions.
6. Consider your geographical area and climate, and also places you may travel to.

What does it cost to wear clothes? Take a look and see!

Garment	Cost	Years of Wear	Months of Wear per Year	Average Times Worn	Cost Each Wearing
Wool Suit	$100–$150	3	8	2 times a week	$ .52–$ .82
Winter Coat	$100–$175	3	5	5 times a week	$ .33–$ .58
Summer Suit	$75–$100	2	4	2 times a week	$1.16–$1.95
Silk Blouse	$30–$60	3	12	1 time a week	$ .21–$ .42
Wool Pants	$30–$80	2	6	1 time a week	$ .62–$1.66
Trendy Sweater	$25–$35	1	6	2 times a week	$2.08–$3.00
Low-Heel Pump	$40–$50	1	12	2 times a week	$ .41–$ .52
Classic Shoe	$40–$80	2	12	2 times a week	$ .26–$ .42

Fill out the chart below with your own budget
in mind:

Notes

How to Read a Fashion Photo or Ad

After the planning is completed for your wardrobe, begin to study fashion magazines and ads, and also the manikins in store windows.

To learn to analyze current fashion, begin by noticing different types of accessories and the use of various fashion lengths. You can learn a great deal by observing how fashion works. Take a pen and go through your favorite fashion magazine, making notes on the new fashions, styles, and tricks. Learning is never over for the woman who wants to look special.

Take a Look

What's at the neck? How is it tied?
Is there jewelry? Where and what style?
A suit? Separates? What textures?
Small or large lapels?
Skirts pleated or straight?
Tops belted, tucked in or out?
Skirt length short or long?
Jacket hip length or waist high?
Hose sheer or opaque, textured or plain?
Are the shoes pumps or sandals? Heel height
　low or high?

　What did you learn? Try this each month as you study a fashion magazine.

What Is Seasonless Dressing?

Seasonless clothing spans the seasons and always looks great, regardless of time or place. Thirty to fifty percent of your clothing should fall into this category.

　There are certain colors that are seasonless: navy, black, beige, white, and red. Choose the colors and fabrics that work best for your climate.

　The best fabrics for unlimited seasonal use are jersey, lightweight wool crepe, lightweight suedes, fine jerseys, crepe de chine or Charmeuse, gabardine, fine cottons, and some flannels.

　Clothes should have no permanent ornamentation.

　Separates are marvelous because they are so versatile. You can interchange a jersey blouse with a skirt or trousers and use your various pieces to the fullest.

　If I were to choose just three items for seasonless dressing, they would be:

a fabulous pair of pants
a cashmere (or similar) dress
a cardigan jacket

Each of the above would be in black, navy, or ivory, for endless dressing!

To plan your future color-coordinated wardrobe, fill in the squares with a description of the color or a fabric swatch. Use only two or three colors that coordinate and completely interchange for the basic versatile pieces of clothing.

Clothing	Color	Color	Color
Coat			
Separates			
Suit			
Pant Set			
Dress			
Accessories			
Accessories			

The Night Before

Plan your clothing needs the night before you need them. Place them all together outside your closet. This eliminates last-minute rushing when you might discover soiled or damaged clothing that you neglected to pull from your closet to repair earlier.

Use this guide to check everything for the next day's wear, or you may wish to prepare a week's clothing in advance.

Blouse

Jewelry

Jacket/Top

Scarf

Dress

Belt

Skirt/Pants

Hosiery

Shoes

Blouse/Sweater

Undergarments

Date _____

Occasion _____

Your Closet– Friend or Foe?

It is pleasant to see plans develop. . . .

Proverbs 13:19

Someone once calculated that most women wear only 10 percent of the items in their wardrobes—90 percent of the time! If this is true, we all probably need to clear out the excess in our closets.

Let's begin by cleaning out the clothes in your closet that you haven't worn for seasons (maybe years). Keep only the clothes you actually wear. Does that sound impossible? You've tried it before? Well, maybe you had no plan in mind, and so you kept many of the would-be discards tucked way back in your closet.

I have a plan for you. It works very well and takes only about an hour to complete. The idea is to weed out the clothes that won't fit into your new "coordinated" look.

When you finish, you will know that what you have will work for you. You will also know what you need to complete your wardrobe, and how much room you have left over.

Take this book with you and lay it on the bed near your closet. Follow these instructions carefully.

Second pile   Clothing that needs to be repaired, cleaned, or altered.

Inventory Time!

Open your closet and take a good, long look. You will never see it like this again. What a relief!

Now take out all of your clothing and place it on your bed. (Make your bed first!)

Begin to separate all your clothing into these three separate piles. (Exclude some seasonal clothing and long gowns that require a formal situation and may not be worn more than once a year.)

Third pile   Clothing that you *actually wear*. (Not what you *want* to wear, but what you *do* wear!)

Every item in your wardrobe should have been placed in one of these three piles. Stop waiting to lose weight so you can wear the clothes that are too small. Once you lose weight, you'll be so excited you'll want to buy new clothes!

What next? Items in pile #1 must be boxed up, taken to a consignment shop, or given to a thrift shop or missionary barrel.

Pile #2 is the closet clutterer—the worst kind of culprit. Put the items that need to be repaired in a box and begin the repairing, cleaning, and altering within a few weeks. If you haven't finished everything within a year,

First pile   Clothing that you haven't worn for one to two years or more or can no longer wear.

discard it all, just as you have done with pile #1. Don't trick yourself into believing that someday you'll get to it!

Now that you've discarded the "losers" you are ready for the "winners." Hopefully, they will be workable for your new look.

Begin to work with pile #3. Separate the clothes by colors, dividing the ones that are best for you from the ones that are not. Organize all of your best colors and put them in your closet, with beiges in one area, blacks in another, and so on. Put the hanging items that are not your best colors in a separate section of the closet. Use them until you are ready to replace them with something in your correct color. (Patience! It took me three years to totally color coordinate my wardrobe!)

Take a good look at what is in your closet. Try on everything. Experiment. If you can coordinate for more than two to four weeks in advance without using the same items, you have too many clothes. You probably won't wear them all. Recently I helped a woman clean out her closet. She had forty pairs of pants and yet "didn't have a thing to wear!"

Now take a long look at the "wearable" clothes hanging in your closet. Is everything black? Gray? Neutral? Yes, your basics may need to be dark or neutral, but you also need some color in your life! This works in reverse, too. If you have too many brights, you'll need basics and neutrals to put it all together. See chapter 3 for your best colors.

Now, take another look. Is your fabric all the same texture? All knit? All silk? All smooth? If so, add a little interesting texture to some of your next selections.

Still another look. Is everything one mood? Tailored? Ruffled and feminine? Variation could be your clue to adding a different dimension to your wardrobe. Just a piece or two could add spice.

One last look does it. But this time it's back to the boxes of discards. Try to analyze why a particular item wasn't used more often. Was it the wrong color? Wrong style? Did it cost too much to clean? Was it a "mistake" purchase and you had nowhere to wear it? Once you've analyzed why you didn't use a particular garment more often, you might notice a pattern you have been following. Try to avoid making the same mistake when shopping in the future.

Handy Hanging

An organized closet can do more for your wardrobe than you realize. To begin with, folding and hanging clothes correctly extends their life span. It prevents static that can contribute to snags and pulls, and it eliminates the need for extra ironing. Organization helps you to see precisely what you have, so you can readily discover all your coordination possibilities.

Always hang clothing items immediately after removing them. Draping garments over the furniture creates wrinkles and can cause fabrics to wear out prematurely. (Not to mention how unsightly the room looks!)

In a special place, hang items that need cleaning or repair. Take care of the repairs as soon as possible, and have items cleaned immediately.

Plastic or ceramic hooks are great for hanging robes and nightgowns. Mug racks hung in your closet or room are terrific for keeping accessories (belts, bags, scarves, and ribbons) in order.

Wire hangers tend to ruin shoulder shapes and often cause snags in fabrics. Try using padded hangers for your best clothing, and rounded plastic hangers for the other items. Hang pants and knit sweaters on the lower, padded part of a hanger. This saves space and helps guard against wrinkles, creases, and hanger marks.

Space-Making Gadgets That Work

Make the most of your closet space with this great organizer. Just one hanger stores six blouses or shirts. It also helps keep them fresh and wrinkle free.

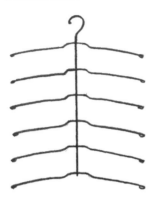

The skirt stacker holds four skirts, and saves space by holding skirts vertically.

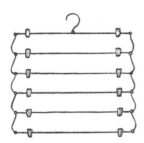

Two plus two equals one? Well, it does with this great pants hanger. Four pairs of pants hang separately and securely. When you shop for this item, make sure each bar is thicker than wire and is vinyl covered. It should also include bars that unfasten so pants are easy to get on and off the gadget.

Organization! That's the name of the game in your closet, and when you play it right, you're playing to make your whole life simpler.

Here's an easy way to put shelves in your closet: Add a quilted vinyl utility chest.

To keep your clothes their freshest, hang a scented deodorizer in the closet; change the scent frequently.

Have you ever wondered why you seem to have only *one* shoe of every kind? Ever been surprised to find a long-lost pair of shoes in a closet corner or under floor-length dresses?

Try these storage tips: Get all your shoes off the floor. This way you won't have to hunt for your shoes among the tangle of clothes near the floor. Install a special narrow shelf to hold shoes and boots. Store your shoes on the back of the closet door in a pocketed shoe bag; or use see-through shoe boxes or clear stacking bins arranged on your top shelf.

Avoid floor shoe racks, as they are difficult to see and reach. Leave the floor space free. Don't use ordinary shoe boxes for shoe storage, as you can't see through them.

Additional Closet Helps

Good lighting is a must for a closet workshop. If yours is poor, get a small battery-operated light. It's easy to install and you will be pleased with the result.

There are always favorite ways of doing things. Here are some of mine, and they all work on *one* bedroom wall:

My accessories (scarves, ties, belts, flowers) are color coordinated, labeled, and put in plastic see-through boxes and stacked in my closet.

My necklaces, pendants, bracelets, and hanging jewelry are arranged by color on clear plastic mug racks on my bedroom wall (reds together, golds, and so forth).

My earrings are in a clear compartment case originally intended for fishing flies. (Your local hardware store probably carries them.)

My lapel pins are in a clear plastic box stacked below my earring box. (Both are on an old bookcase.)

My large belts, divided by color, are on a colored pegboard on the bedroom wall behind the door.

Belts, ties, chains, beads, and hats can be put on poles designed to hang plants. For hats and scarves, large ceramic hooks on a wall work nicely.

The Seasonal Spruce-Up

If it's time for the seasonal switch of clothing and accessories, simplify the task. When putting away last season's clothes, go through your closet and drawers, room by room, with grocery bags labeled as follows: "give away," "throw away," "repair," and "save." Place articles in appropriate bags.

Repair damaged items. Clean everything, laundering washables and dry cleaning others. Don't put anything away until it is clean and dry. Soil can weaken fibers.

Hang items in plastic bags or fold and put in boxes. Seldom-worn garments should be kept in fabric bags to keep them clean. The same goes for items which pick up lint and dust readily. Plastic dry cleaners' bags used for long periods of time, however, can create mildew in some fabrics.

Label boxes so you know what's inside. Keep sweaters and jackets handy for the first chill of fall. Keep gloves, scarves, and hats together.

Boots, shoes, and handbags of man-made materials should be washed with a sudsy sponge, rinsed, and dried. Use a special

cleaner and polish on leather. Stuff boots, shoes, and bags with paper to help them retain their shape. Store them in boxes. Old socks make good protective shoe bags. Never store leather bags, boots, or shoes in plastic. Leather, like silk and down fabrics, must breathe. Boot trees in your boots prevent tops from bending over and creasing.

If storage space is a problem, see if your dry cleaner will store some items. Some cleaners will store clothes for the price of cleaning them. If your cleaner won't do this, or if the price is too high, store the out-of-season clothing in cardboard boxes made to slide under your bed. I know a woman who covered her boxes with fabric and used them as end tables in a spare bedroom.

If there is room in your closet to hang both summer and winter clothes, hang the unused clothing toward the back. Furs should be professionally stored, as they need consistent temperature and humidity that your closet cannot provide.

With your closets and drawers empty, it might be a good time to freshen everything. Be creative as you wash and paint. Possibly you can create new space dividers or shelf storage.

Reline drawers with paper or vinyl. Now you're ready to unpack and use next season's apparel and accessories.

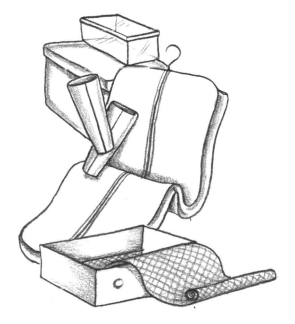

Creative

Coordination

Good sense is far more valuable than gold or
precious jewels.

Proverbs 20:15

With most of the planning behind us, we can
now look forward to the fun of coordinating.

You have analyzed your figure, know your
correct colors, and have planned your wardrobe. With your life-style in mind, check the
basic pieces you need to *complete* your
wardrobe coordination. Select only one or
two items in each category. If you don't,
you'll have too many clothes, "nothing to
wear," and a closetful of frustration!

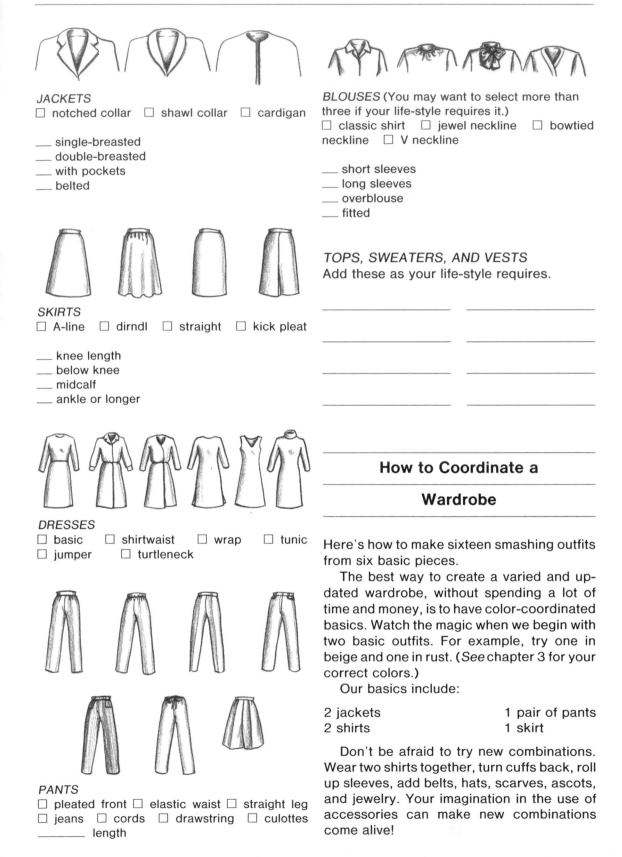

JACKETS
☐ notched collar   ☐ shawl collar   ☐ cardigan

___ single-breasted
___ double-breasted
___ with pockets
___ belted

BLOUSES (You may want to select more than three if your life-style requires it.)
☐ classic shirt   ☐ jewel neckline   ☐ bowtied neckline   ☐ V neckline

___ short sleeves
___ long sleeves
___ overblouse
___ fitted

TOPS, SWEATERS, AND VESTS
Add these as your life-style requires.

_____   _____

_____   _____

_____   _____

_____   _____

SKIRTS
☐ A-line   ☐ dirndl   ☐ straight   ☐ kick pleat

___ knee length
___ below knee
___ midcalf
___ ankle or longer

DRESSES
☐ basic   ☐ shirtwaist   ☐ wrap   ☐ tunic
☐ jumper   ☐ turtleneck

PANTS
☐ pleated front ☐ elastic waist ☐ straight leg
☐ jeans   ☐ cords   ☐ drawstring   ☐ culottes
_____ length

How to Coordinate a
Wardrobe

Here's how to make sixteen smashing outfits from six basic pieces.

The best way to create a varied and up-dated wardrobe, without spending a lot of time and money, is to have color-coordinated basics. Watch the magic when we begin with two basic outfits. For example, try one in beige and one in rust. (*See* chapter 3 for your correct colors.)

Our basics include:

2 jackets	1 pair of pants
2 shirts	1 skirt

Don't be afraid to try new combinations. Wear two shirts together, turn cuffs back, roll up sleeves, add belts, hats, scarves, ascots, and jewelry. Your imagination in the use of accessories can make new combinations come alive!

Sample Budget of Six Pieces

Approximate cost to make:

light-colored wool-blend jacket	$ 30
dark-colored all-wool jacket	40
wool-blend skirt	20
polyester/wool/gabardine pants	30
1 cotton/polyester shirt	20
1 silk-look blouse	20
Total cost	$160

Sixteen days of changes equals only ten dollars a day!!

The Perfect Student Wardrobe (Ideal for Any Teenager)

No one is more aware of both the trials and pleasures of dressing than college students today. Many of them are working as well as studying, so a well-planned wardrobe is even more essential.

Twenty-one pieces of clothing can get you started and give you over fifty different looks—enough clothes for at least four years of wear!

Let's begin with a numbered list of the clothing items. You will find the corresponding numbers next to the illustrations. Study the illustrations and discover the many changes available to you. (A color example is given in each case.)

1. blazer (gray)
2. skirt to match blazer
3. pants to match blazer
4. sweater vest (pale gray)
5. sweater cardigan (berry)
6. jeans (navy)
7. plaid kilt skirt (berry/blue/white)
8. long skirt (black)
9. dressy jersey top (black)
10. turtleneck sweater (bright blue)
11. V-neck sweater (white)
12. bowed silk-look blouse (white)
13. menswear-styled shirt (light blue)
14. plaid shirt (matches kilt colors)
15. velvet pants (black)
16. jogging jacket (hot pink)
17. jogging pants (hot pink)
18. sweater dress (light taupe)
19. large ''sweep'' shawl (multicolored)
20. shirtwaist silk-look blouse (plum)
21. ski jacket (wine/blue)

1,2,20,4   1,3,10   1,3,4,14   2,18   2,4,14   2,9   1,2,12   1,2,10,19   2,20,19   10,3

2,5,12   3,14,5   1,3,13   3,4,9   18   18,3   1,18   18,7   18,20   18,19

11,13,7　13,7　5,11,7　13,5,7　14,7,10　14,7,4　7,12　7,10　7,11　7,20,21

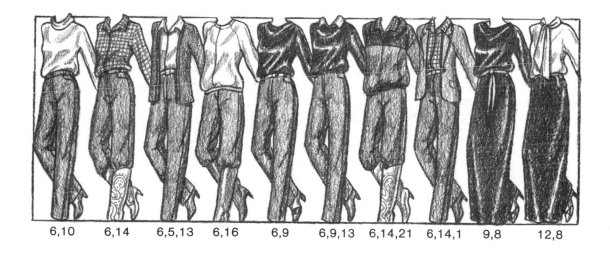

6,10　6,14　6,5,13　6,16　6,9　6,9,13　6,14,21　6,14,1　9,8　12,8

20,8,19　8,19　8,19　4,8,20　9,15　10,15,19　15,5,14　15,20　16,15　16,17

Coats, Anyone?

Every wardrobe should contain at least one coat. Many women have questions about the selection of such an important item. When shopping for a coat, choose a solid color and basic style. If your budget only allows for one, choose a simple trench coat. It will work for almost all occasions, year-round. One trench style is shown on our model. Consider your figure. Should you wear a belted style or not? Are shoulder details for you? Consider all the options, and consult chapter 4 on figure solutions for your correct choice.

Since your budget may not stretch to include additional coats, your basic coat should have a zip-in lining of a warm fabric. This can be removed during warmer weather. For the warm-season woman, the coat should be camel color, for the cool-season person, taupe. These colors are best for the greatest versatility year-round.

Check your best coat color (refer also to chapter 3 on color).
taupe _____
camel _____

Summer Essentials

Plan a summer wardrobe with a few essentials. Start with six basic pieces. The key is to keep everything in two colors (for example, navy and white). Add accessories for updating. The classic looks in your basic six items should work interchangeably. All you'll need are the proper accessories to make your look new and fashionable for each summer.

Here are the six basic items:

cotton tunic dress (for example, white)
simple linen suit (white)
pullover sweater (navy and white)
linen shorts (white)
two-piece, tiny-print, short-sleeved silk dress (navy and white)
a white broadcloth shirt to wear under it all

Have fun with accessories!

Dressing for Two (Your Pregnancy Wardrobe)

Looking back, I remember wanting to buy maternity clothes the moment I learned I was pregnant! But, how soon the novelty wore off! Nine months is a long time to live in maternity smocks. Thank goodness times have changed, and women now have more choices in maternity clothing. There really are some delightful new looks.

Here are my suggestions for a good-looking pregnancy wardrobe:

1 jumper (wear it alone or with tops)
1 tunic jacket (as a cover-up for the first few months and a suit look later on)
2 skirts
2 casual smocks

1 pair light-colored corduroy slacks
1 long tunic cardigan sweater
1 pair "painter" overalls (the kind that expand as you do!)
1 pair black faille evening pants
1 pair gray flannel slacks
1 pair bright-colored sweat pants (It's great just to loosen the drawstring!)

All comfortable and fun!

Dressing tip: Concentrate on small places—neck, wrist, and ankles—and on new accessories.

The Lucky Twelve

I love to sew. Do you? Because I like quality and good looks, plus a good fit, my first choice is Vogue patterns.

I've mentioned using solid colors for your main staples throughout the last eight chap-

ters. Let's add a little spice and see all the zesty looks that can be found when working with a two-piece plaid dress and Vogue patterns.

Clothing pieces courtesy of Butterick Fashion Marketing Company, New York.

How to Be a
Successful
Shopper

"Utterly worthless!" says the buyer as [she] haggles over the price. But afterwards [she] brags about [her] bargain!

Proverbs 20:14

Erma Bombeck once said:

> One of the secrets of a happy marriage is knowing what your level of tolerance is for one another. Some couples can hang wallpaper together and stay married. Others can back up a recreational van as a team. A few can hang a picture as one. I personally have never been able to shop with my husband and sleep in the same bed with him that night. I couldn't fit all the hostility in the room if I opened the window.

Whether you enjoy shopping alone or with someone, and whether it is a chore or a delight, lies in your motivation.

I shop because I literally love to do it! To me it's relaxing and sometimes is the escape I need from a very busy schedule. While my husband likes to play golf, my recreation is shopping! Even window-shopping can be a great pastime, and also can be very educational in influencing future purchases. Before we begin with the how-tos of shopping, let's determine what kind of shopper you are.

The next time you step into a store, stop and think a moment. Do you know that your buying habits reflect not only your self-discipline but also the way you feel about yourself? Your self-worth is on display for all to see!

Look at your shopping habits. Do you buy out of an emotional need, or do you shop after careful consideration of your needs?

If the major part of your shopping is done from emotional need, you will find that your closet probably does not contain what you need to present a positive image to the world. Often the wardrobe of an emotional shopper is a disaster.

Far-out Fran is an example of an emotional shopper. She has a need to wear clothes that are attention getters. Her wardrobe consists of conspicuous, faddish, far-out clothes which are often out of place. She feels that she cannot be accepted on any other terms. Her wardrobe is a disaster, as fads are not workable or lasting.

Shabby Stella is another shopper who shops out of emotional needs. She will never shop at quality stores or purchase medium or high-price clothes—even though she can afford it! She doesn't even bother to look in better stores because subconsciously she doesn't believe she is worth the higher prices. Her self-image is low, so therefore she looks more poorly dressed than necessary. In reality, she ends up spending more money because her less-expensive clothing wears out more quickly than quality fabrics.

There are many other types of emotional shoppers. Look at your habits, try to determine how to shop more on a rational basis, and you'll learn how to be a wise shopper.

Be tasteful and modest in your buying habits, and your money will go further. Being a good steward of your money takes discipline. Discipline and self-worth go hand in hand. "He who neglects [lacks] discipline despises himself . . ." (Proverbs 15:32 NASB).

To begin to learn about successful shopping, let's take a peek into our favorite store window.

The Art of Window-Shopping

Window-shopping costs nothing and can be lots of fun. When I window-shop I take a small note pad and a pencil and jot down my observations.

I strive to answer the following:

1. Are certain combinations of fabrics appearing regularly? How?
2. What is the silhouette you see most often?
3. What's the length in skirts, pants, jackets, and coats?
4. What colors are current? How are they used in combination?
5. What color stockings are being used? Are they textured?

6. Are accessories small or large?
7. What's the width of belts? What about styles? Colors? Fabrics? Buckles?
8. What's the look in handbags?
9. Are scarves being used? How?
10. Check out the jewelry. What size? Texture? Material?
11. Learn ways to coordinate up-to-date looks.
12. Is the store fashion trendy or conservative? Sophisticated? Junior?
13. Remember that everything you see doesn't necessarily mean it's "in," or it's for you. Common sense is the key.

After you have planned your wardrobe and listed your needs on the charts in chapter 6, you are ready to begin shopping.

Following are a few important things to consider before you leave for that adventure.

Just as you should never go grocery shopping when you are hungry, don't go clothes shopping when you feel "down." Depression will emphasize all your defects and negative points such as bulges. The way you shop will be more positive if you do it when you're feeling good about yourself. Not everything will look fabulous, but *many* things will!

Look through fashion magazines and examine new trends. Study what the experts are doing with clothing for the current season. But remember, don't overdo trendy clothing.

Have you ever wondered what the difference is between a "fad" and a "trend"? A fad is something that comes into style quickly and goes out just as fast. It doesn't actually affect the flow of fashion.

A trend, or trendy influence, does affect fashion and can be included in a successfully dressed woman's attire in *small amounts.* If dresses have been full, and now the silhouette is closer to the body, her garments may be altered to a degree. Trends often indicate future mainstays of fashion.

For example, if the trendy look is the tunic, simply add a tunic look to your wardrobe— just one, not three (unless your budget allows for it).

A silky tunic can be worn over a skirt and later added over silk evening pants. (To be a truly trendy dresser one must have an expansive pocketbook!)

Attending fashion shows will help prepare you for the latest fashions. It can also increase your knowledge of what to add or delete from your closet for the current season. At a dramatic fashion show that is selling a new look, the designers may try to attract the potential consumer by whatever means possible. They often grossly exaggerate runway renditions of fashions in order to shock the public into noticing. It's been said that the madder the runway goings-on, the more likely the show will make headlines. And often what appears in the newspapers and on television screens is what sells clothing.

So attend a couple of fashion shows a year (fall-winter and spring-summer), and watch with tongue-in-cheek and a little humor!

Take your list of shopping needs with you, and then shop only for the items on that list. And have your "wardrobe on a safety pin." In the eight years I have used this system, I have saved countless hours that might have been spent in returning items that turned out to be the wrong color. Here's how it works: Snip a small piece of fabric from a seam or hem of a garment that you wear. Pick a spot where there is no extra pull or stretch. Or you can use a scrap from your sewing room. Put all the pieces on a one-and-one-half-inch-wide safety pin and tuck it into a small, clear plastic bag. Take this with you wherever you go.

If you know your correct colors, you may also want to carry your color-analysis card with you. (*See* chapter 3 and the order form at back of this book.)

Hold on a moment! Remember to look *before you buy!*

Be a professional shopper and take a "looking" trip before you buy. Susan, a friend from my fashion-modeling days, is a buyer for a large department-store chain. She will not buy anything until she takes a "shopping the market" trip. She recommends: Do some exploring; learn to com-

pare; go to *all* price-range shops, from dis-
counts to designers, to see what's available.

As a discriminating shopper look for fabrics, sizes, styles, colors, workmanship
(quality), price range, special display sections, and manikins. Ask yourself, "Why
does this dress look better? Why is it more
expensive?" Educate yourself on the whys
and hows of quality and price.

You might try looking at the merchandise
at a discount store and comparing it to the
clothing at I. Magnin or Saks Fifth Avenue.
Can you see the difference? (Not just the
price difference!) In this way, you will
broaden your understanding and prepare
yourself for future purchasing.

Try on a few things, as Susan said, from
designer brands to discount merchandise.
Do you wear a size 8 in one brand and a 12 in
another?

After the fun (or frustration?) of this
"looking trip," go back to the clothing in your
closet and you will see your present wardrobe from a new perspective. But be positive!
There is hope! Remember, you are going to
build your wardrobe with basics and add
flare only in touches you learned about
through your window-shopping.

Ask Yourself

What have I learned from this trip?
What should I expect in prices?
Where should I shop?
What shops seemed interested in me as a
    customer?
What shop was too trendy?
Where did I see quality merchandise?

With a written list of your wardrobe needs,
your fabric swatches, your color-analysis
card, notes about what is correct for your figure, plus information on cost and quality of
clothing, where to shop, and how much you
have to spend—you are ready to begin!

Remember to

buy with *your* image in mind (total picture)
buy to complete what you already have for
    that total look
buy what you like, and feel good in
buy seasonless clothing (whenever possible)

Shop for clothes that serve more than one
purpose.

Use This *Magic Three*

Can I wear it to *three* different events?
Does it go with at least *three* outfits presently
    in my closet?
Can I wear it for at least *three* years, and will
    it still look like a quality garment?
Can it be accessorized at least *three* differ-
    ent ways?

Buy the best you can afford! Good-quality
fabrics and merchandise will last a long time.
(*See* pages 109, 110 for quality finds.)

To insure true wardrobe versatility, purchase only clothing that is free of contrasting
color in topstitching, heavy details, and frills.
Stick with neutral and basic colors for the
main wardrobe selections. Shop for color in
less expensive items such as blouses, belts,
and scarves. Don't purchase anything until
you first look at yourself in a three-way mirror! Even a handbag should not be purchased until you see yourself full length
holding it.

Learn where and when the seasonal bargains are to be found. (*See* page 111.)

Remember that accessories can trans-
form your look. When buying a fabric, drape
it around your shoulders and neck, and
check the color effect in a full-length mirror.

*Remember, shop only with a written list of
clothing needs, and buy only what is on your
list!*

If absolutely necessary you may, to begin with, ask a friend to go shopping with you. That friend *must* be a person whom you respect and who knows about good wardrobe practices. It's better, however, to shop alone so you will learn how to make good choices.

If you purchase an outfit and then aren't certain whether it was a wise choice, hang it *outside* your wardrobe closet and decide within seven days whether to keep it or not. Most stores will take back merchandise if you have the receipt and return the item within seven days. If you find an outfit is really not good for you, don't be hesitant to return it. Be assertive!

Miscellaneous Reminders

and Suggestions

1. Before you go shopping, take time to read ads and fashion magazines. Know what is happening in your area.
2. Make a list of what you want to look for.
3. Find a role model—at work, where you attend church, or at a club meeting. Analyze her hair, makeup, and clothing. Try to discover why she looks so smashing.
4. Be yourself and trust your intuition. You know when you feel good in certain garments.
5. Shop only in the stores that you know sell your style.
6. Find a store that you feel relates to you and your life-style.
7. Select a salesperson with whom you have good rapport and who knows your taste.
8. When trying on clothing, look at your whole figure—head to toe, back to front.
9. Choose clothing that works for more than one kind of event.
10. Don't shop when you are in a rush. Take time. Ask yourself key questions such as "Will I be able to wear this next year?"
11. Buy quality, but look for bargain prices.
12. Have garments altered to fit you perfectly.
13. When buying jewelry, select something that says *you*, a one-of-a-kind piece in good taste.

Discount Shopping

Are you interested in saving money and looking good? Discount shopping may be the answer for you.

I have purchased many staples for my wardrobe through discount stores and have sometimes paid 50 percent or less for many designer items.

You must be prepared before you tackle discount shopping, or the whole experience can be very frustrating.

Most discount stores have miles and miles of racks crammed with clothing. The dressing rooms are less than appealing and never private, and the crowds can be awesome. But the shopping will usually be very rewarding—if you are *prepared*. Do a little planning on what you'd like to look for, but also be open for good bargains.

Loehmann's and Marshall's are two of the many discount shopping stores across the United States that offer savings of 20 percent to 60 percent and up.

I'll never forget my first experience with discount-store shopping, at Filene's Basement in Boston. There were no dressing rooms, and the women were dressing (and undressing) in the aisles. But the prices (and the fun) were well worth the extra effort required in fighting the crowds. I've often purchased all items on my Christmas list in one day's shopping at Filene's Basement, and saved over 50 percent on all purchases! I've found $40 sleepwear for $3, designer blouses for $15, and even a $150 evening gown for $7.50!

From all my learning experiences, here are some ideas that I gleaned, and a few suggestions for you.

Wear comfortable shoes and a slightly flared skirt that slips on and off easily, with no buttons or zippers. I prefer a skirt instead of pants so I can try on a pair of pants under my skirt if there is no dressing room. Wear a buttonless slipover top. You might wear a stretchy one-piece undergarment to give you a smooth line and a little more cover-up for the communal dressing rooms!

If possible, tuck a pair of heels in your handbag, as you may need them to get the "feel" of what some garments will look like when worn with a dressier shoe.

Don't wear any jewelry except a watch.

Sometimes it's helpful to have a friend along. She can gather items for you—a different size, color, and so forth. You can help each other.

If you find something that you like, buy it! If it goes back on the rack, it probably will be gone when you return later to buy it.

Take your correct color swatches with you so you can get the best match. Often the merchandise cannot be returned.

Prior to your shopping day, you might phone the store and ask which days the merchandise arrives and is displayed in the bargain department. These will be the best shopping days, as the merchandise will not be too badly picked over. Ask if you must pay cash or if credit cards are accepted.

Shopping when the store first opens is helpful.

Matching skirts and blouses are not always on the same rack. If you find a "perfect" blouse, keep looking. You may find the matching skirt on another rack.

Don't be in a hurry when you discount shop. It takes time to prowl through hundreds of skirts and dresses and then wait in line to make your purchase.

Be particularly careful about sizes, as the tags are sometimes misleading. I have purchased anything from a size 6 to a size 12 and had them all fit well. Try the garment on if it looks as if it could fit. You might be pleasantly surprised.

Now, one last word of warning. Be on guard against bargain fever. It's easy to buy more than you really need.

Sometimes the difference between an expensive item and a not-so-expensive item is just the label, and sometimes it's quality and style.

Discount stores often cut out labels, and you will just have to guess the designer's name. But the Federal Trade Commission has now assigned identification numbers to manufacturers, and by law, these numbers must be on all designers' garments. Here are a few ID numbers of favorite designers:

Act 1: RN36486, RN36789, RN51331
Anne Klein: RN40803
Bill Blass: RN38344
Bobbie Brooks: RN47302
Charlotte Ford: RN43163, RN50003
Calvin Klein: RN41327, RN42642
Evan-Picone: RN35685, WPL08582
Geoffrey Beene Inc.: RN33293
Halston Originals Inc.: RN46616
Jantzen: RN37966, WPL06979
Jonathan Logan: RN34972, RN44290, RN43232, WPL09442

Lilli Ann: RN14962, RN29563
Liz Claiborne: RN52002
Perry Ellis: RN57272
Ralph Lauren Originals: RN56158
Sassoon: RN54516
Stanley Blacker: RN30219, RN41550, RN55639, WPL11388, WPL11390
Villager: RN17470, RN31242

You may go to your local library and ask for the *RN & WPL Directory* to obtain additional codes.

Finding Quality Clothing

To find the best buys for your dollar, look for these quality signs:

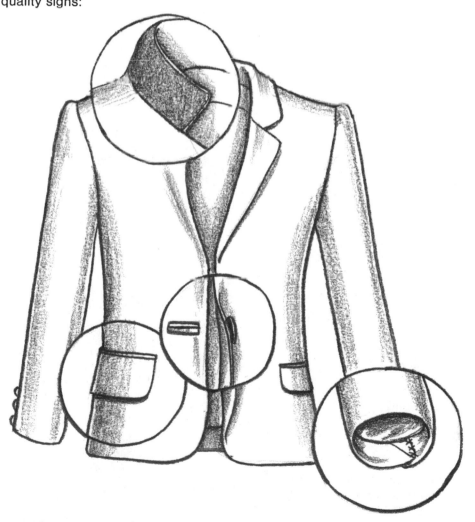

generous seam allowances and hems

raw edges finished to prevent raveling

plaids and stripes matched precisely at the seams

underlining throughout garment for holding shape and preventing seams and darts from pulling the fabric

collars and lapels that stand up, roll, or lie flat because they have a built-in shape of their own

collars that are constructed so that the top turns slightly over the edges, hiding the undercollar

crisp, sturdy interfacings that spring back into shape after you crumple the garment in your hand

quality zippers and buttons

closely woven seam tapes, face, or lace bindings

a separate lining attached to the inside of the garment in various places to cover raw edges and to provide a completely finished interior

---

"Menswear tailoring" is quality tailoring. Often you can find a woman's jacket or coat in such tailoring. Here are the things to look for:

underside of collar is faced with felt, and collar hangs smoothly

buttonholes are bound

the knotting on buttons is done through outer layer of fabric only

pockets and tabs are finished to lie flat, no bulk

seam allowances on cuffs are generous, and fabric is folded under, not cut on hem

Don't Buy Clothing With

a neckline that gapes or shoulders that droop; these are signs that the garment is too big at the shoulders or upper chest above the bust line; this is an area of the garment that can't be corrected without the enlargement of an already too-large armhole

a hemline on a sharply pleated skirt that is too short, so that if you let the hem down you will never get rid of the original crease

a dart or seam that has been punctured or clipped at the stitching line

a dress that is too short waisted and hasn't enough seam allowance to be lowered

a garment of synthetic or synthetic-blend fabric (except knits) that needs to be let out at seams or hem, as often original creases cannot be pressed out of such fabrics

Ideal Times for Buying Clothing

January
leather boots
winter coats
furs
fabrics
after-five dresses
winter clothing
handbags
jewelry
shoes

February
men's clothing
winter shoes
furs

March
winter clothing
furs

April
spring clothes
furs
children's clothes
dresses
men's suits
fabrics
spring coats

May
spring sportswear
handbags

June
men's suits
men's socks
underwear
shoes

July
handbags
shoes, sandals
swimsuits
summer clothing

August
furs
summer clothes
handbags

September
(*not* a good
month to buy
back-to-school
clothes)

October
coats
lingerie
hosiery
autumn clothing
wools, wool blends

November
winter coats
winter suits

December
Before Christmas:
   men's suits
   men's coats
After Christmas:
   fantastic buys
   in designer clothes
   in high-fashion
   stores—sales in all
   departments!

   The smart shopper will know when to buy to save money. January and February are the best bargain times. June and December are the worst. Try to buy items that are slightly off-season, as that is when the retailer needs to clear the floors for new merchandise.

The Indispensables

> Friendly suggestions are as pleasant as per-
> fume.
>
> Proverbs 27:9

Accessories are like the icing on the cake.
They add sparkle to clothes. Accessories
can change a look from day to evening or
from winter to summer, and they are an inexpensive way of updating your basics for
the new looks of the season.

If you have avoided using accessories
because you didn't know how to use them,
you won't go wrong if you follow certain
guidelines regarding color and coordination.
The important thing is that you try them. And
while trying, remember to wear only what is
correct for *your* body size and proportions.
You'll like them, and so will everyone else!

Shoes, scarves, belts, jewelry, hosiery,
hats, and gloves are the necessary items to
complete your accessory collection.

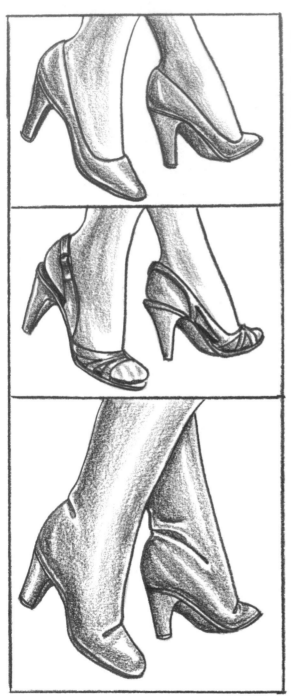

Shoes

Your wardrobe should include shoes that fit your life-style. A working woman often needs different styles from those of the woman at home, or the student.

Pumps are good year-round, while sandals will be worn more in the warm weather and for evening.

Your shoes should be the same color, or darker, than the hem of your pants, dress, or skirt. For a very casual, sporty look, you may go brighter, but you should repeat that bright color in a scarf or a piece of colorful jewelry.

A few suggested styles are as follows:

basic pair of pumps in a dark or neutral color for year-round use

sandals for warm weather and evening wear—you may wear them in some office situations, depending on the climate and working conditions

leather boots with a medium heel for wet, cold weather; if you wear boots to work, have a simple pair of work shoes to change into

slingbacks can be a good addition, also

I recommend that you buy only leather. The cost per wearing and the quality look will make your purchase worthwhile.

"When are white shoes worn?" is a question asked by almost everyone. White shoes should be worn only with a predominantly white outfit and usually only in the warm months (bridal and athletic shoes are the exceptions). Also, a sandal might be more flattering to your foot than an all-white, closed pump.

Shoe Care

When buying shoes, remember that quality always pays off in the long run.

To protect your shoes try these ideas:

Look for a protective silicone spray at your shoe-repair store. These sprays are good for both boots and shoes.

Shoe trees will help prolong the life of your boots and shoes. The adjustable kind are best. Insert them after each wearing.

Clean shoes carefully before polishing. Use a good paste polish and lots of elbow grease. Liquid polish is not as good for leather as paste, even though it's easier to use.

If you get caught in a rainstorm and your shoes get wet, stuff them with newspaper and let them dry naturally. Don't put them near a heater, as this may crack the leather. When shoes are completely dry, put them on shoe trees and polish with a good paste.

You might try mink or linseed oil to nourish leather and keep it soft and pliable. Test first, as it might darken the color of light leather slightly.

Salt stains should be washed off immediately with a solution of half white vinegar and half water. Salt can eat into leather.

Suede shoes need special care. Rub an art gum eraser *gently* over the shoe, and then use an emery board with a very soft touch to bring back the pile.

Have nylon taps put on the heels of your shoes to protect them. (Nylon will not make tap-dancing noises.)

Don't wear shoes more than one day without alternating. Airing them out will prolong the life of the shoes.

Your shoes and stockings must "work" together. For example, a heavy-textured stocking can complement the mood of a country casual shoe. And the more feminine the shoe, the more delicate and sheer the hosiery should be.

Don't wear red shoes with navy hose unless you are after a latest trendy look, and you plan to complete that look from head to toe.

For the winter months, when darker hosiery may be desired, it's still best to have the color of hose match the shoe. If you wear black hose, wear black shoes. With brown shoes, wear brown hose (unless you are wearing light-colored clothing).

The most important thing to remember is that your hem color, shoe, and hosiery color should all blend and work together. (No fighting allowed!)

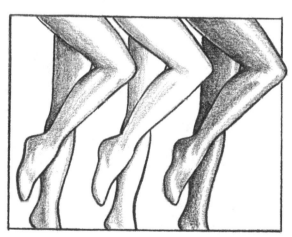

Hosiery

In selecting hosiery, try to make your complete look blend together. Your shoe and hose color should blend. Contrasting color will shorten and emphasize width of legs. (Fashion trends will deviate from the rules in some cases.)

For an all-around color, use a shade that is darker than your natural skin color.

Handbags

Shoes and bags need not necessarily match in color but should blend in fabric. They should both be in an all-purpose color in the same color family.

Leather can be used year-round; straw and linen are for warm months. Leather and suede are a good match in shoes and bag. They work well together.

Select your bag according to your height and weight. A large shoulder bag will look ridiculous on a short girl.

When buying a bag, try it on in front of a full-length mirror. Check the length of the bag to make sure it falls at the proper point. A bag touching at the largest part of the thigh or hip can emphasize a full hip area.

Remove unnecessary clutter from your bag as often as needed. Overstuffing can look sloppy.

Good-quality handbags, like shoes, last longer. And here again, comparison shopping will help you choose the best buy for you.

A Bag Wardrobe Should Include

a medium-size leather shoulder bag for daytime

a leather clutch for all-purpose, year-round
use

an evening bag in silver or gold (according to
your color season)

Following are some pointers to remember
when buying a handbag:

1. Take time to feel the difference in texture of leathers and vinyls.

2. Remember that double stitching indicates durability.

3. Rivets that reinforce the lining under the
leather are advantageous.

4. Those tiny studs on the bottom will protect the bag from scuffs.

5. Pockets on the inside should extend to
the bottom of the bag so there won't be
bulges.

6. Be sure straps have at least a one-half-
inch seam allowance.

Belts

A versatile belt wardrobe will complement
your outfits from month to month, regardless
of the season.

The width of a belt will depend on your
figure and its proportions. Review chapter 4
for the belt width that is best for you.

Choose several styles and looks. A basic
or classic look is the one-inch, good-quality
leather belt.

Select most of your belts in neutral and
basic colors. Then add bright colors for a
fashion look.

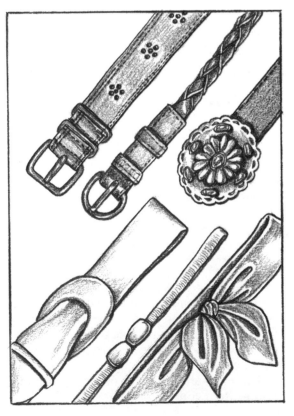

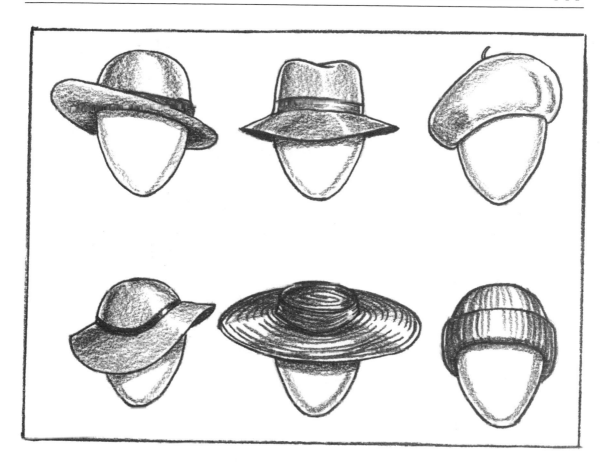

Hats

With the exception of rain, beach, and straw hats, as a rule we aren't seeing women in hats as often as in years past.

When you are buying a hat, be sure to try it on in front of a full-length mirror, taking into consideration your own proportions.

For example, a large-brimmed hat will be overpowering and overwhelming on a five-foot, two-inch woman. The same rule applies when a heavyset woman wears a tiny pillbox hat. Neither hat is correct for either woman!

Keep the hat color the same as the neckline of your garment (or lighter). There will be exceptions, of course, but as a rule this is a good guide to follow.

Wear a hat only if it is appropriate. I know a woman who wears a hat to *all* events. Often it's not appropriate. Obviously, a hat has become her security blanket rather than a fashion symbol.

Hats do make a strong statement, and since I don't enjoy being put into a mold the minute I walk into a room, I don't wear many hats. Often they draw excessive attention, and sometimes that's not what I want, either.

Felt is a year-round fabric for hats. Straw and linen are for spring and summer; feathers, fur, and velvet for the winter months. Velvet is used mainly for evening hours.

Gloves

Gloves are no longer on the necessity list. With a hat, gloves are the perfect touch, however. Gloves should be the same color as the sleeve, or lighter, so as not to draw attention. A pair of good leather gloves in a basic color, and one pair of warm wool gloves, should be adequate. A light-colored summer glove and a longer evening glove are nice for those gala

evening times. Avoid pastel or bright-colored gloves, as they are not a good dollar investment.

Scarves

Scarves . . . how marvelous! My favorite accessory. Scarves are a wonderful way to bring that "best" color to your face while you are waiting to replace the not-so-good colors in your wardrobe.

Everyone can wear scarves, regardless of age or size. Keep your proportions in mind. (*See* chapter 4 for "neck" solutions.)

Let's have some fun with a few of the many ways to work with scarves.

Don't   Short Person   Do

Don't   Full-Figured Person   Do

Jewelry

Selecting jewelry can be a beautiful experience. Choose pieces in relation to your coloring and the colors you have chosen to work with.

For example, to select the very best colors use these guidelines:

If you are a cool-season person your jewelry colors can be silver, platinum, white gold, metal, rose gold; white or pink tones are best in pearls.

If you are a warm-season person, you can select yellow golds, coppers, green golds, ivory, woods; pearls are best in yellow tones.

Jewelry is a very important part of your total wardrobe picture. A pair of earrings is perhaps your most important piece of jewelry. Choose simple ones without dangles Also select a good gold bracelet or two, and a few gold or silver chains to accent your wardrobe look.

You will want to have a new fashionable piece of jewelry for each season to update all your basic pieces. This should be more of a trendy fun piece that can be worn in the evenings or for daytime, depending on your lifestyle.

Save most of your sparkly pins, earrings, and necklaces (similar to rhinestones) for the after-five hours.

Choose jewelry to enhance your outfits. Wear sporty-type jewelry with jeans and tailored jewelry with a basic suit.

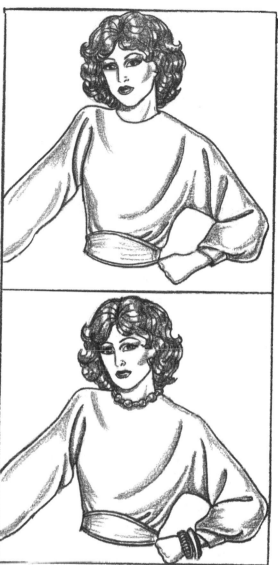

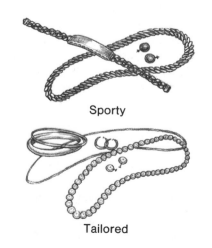

Sporty

Tailored

Notes on Accessory Colors

According to the three basic colors that you decide to use in coordinating your wardrobe, select only two colors of shoes. It isn't necessary to have many colors. Here are some suggestions to take into consideration:

For the Cool-Season Person

summer months: taupe, light gray, or navy sandals
winter months: black, navy, dark gray, chocolate brown, or burgundy pumps

For the Warm-Season Person

summer months: light camel, rust, or brown sandals
winter months: brown, rust, camel, or royal navy pumps

Fill in the following, using your season and wardrobe colors as guides:

My two pairs of shoe colors will include summertime: _____   _____

wintertime: _____   _____

Choose only one color for the spring/summer months and one for the winter months for your handbags. This color should blend with your entire wardrobe. I choose a dark, basic color for the cold months and a lighter, neutral color for the warm months.

My handbag color for summertime:

_____

My handbag color for wintertime:

_____

Updating: How Do You Do It?

Update your wardrobe at least every six months. Make a list of your needs. List the accessories you'll need to update for the new season. Study the mistakes you have made in the past and try to avoid making them in the future.

Instant change: *day* into *evening* clothing. It's not that difficult. Accessories do it for you!

(1) The evening updater: sequins, the cardigan jacket, and T-shirt in hot colors.
(2) Newest silk blouse: gilded metallics with ruffles, or in stripes.
(3) Basic evening jewelry: bracelets and earrings in black and gold——they cover all bases.
(4) Shoes to collect: the evening sandal, the closed pump.
(5) Camisoles: the best tops for the new dinner suits; go for texture news in angora and metallic sparkle, worn under a jacket.
(6) Belts: the new conversation pieces—— beaded suede, gold mesh, important buckles, with slim skirts.

How to Dress for Seven Days in a Versatile Dress— Seven Different Ways

Did you know that your "seven-day wonder dress" may very well be hanging right in your closet? The marvelous classic shirtwaist dress! Study the seven versatile ways to wear the dress (including the Saturday-evening date), and then go to your closet and see what you can do!

Monday

Tuesday

Wednesday

Thursday

Friday

Saturday

Sunday

What to Wear–
When and Where

Be prepared—all dressed and ready. . . .

Luke 12:35

One of the most important questions asked about wardrobe is regarding which outfit to wear for a specific occasion.

Following are some guidelines to make you feel confident and comfortable wherever you go!

In the Suburbs or a Small Town

For a position outside the home, for community activities, and for shopping, choose simple, well-cut, flattering dresses in bright tones, and suits in tweeds. And of course you need a coat to wear over everything (camel's hair, tweed, or classic trench coat). Include tweed or flannel skirts and blouses and pull-on or cardigan sweaters. Pants are optional, depending on how informal or casual your occasion is. For club and community meetings, a dress or suit is always good. For teas and afternoon or Sunday events, wear an afternoon dress in either wool or silk, simply cut and not too elaborate. Accessories should be in keeping with the mood of your clothes.

For evening social life you may be a little more daring, wearing culottes, evening pajamas, pants, and decorative sweaters and tops. You may wear these to other homes, or in your own home for dinners. For family occasions or dining at home, wear comfortable lounge wear such as pants or a long hostess dress. For informal evenings with friends or at dinner (daytime or afternoon), dresses are appropriate.

In the Medium-Sized City to

the Metropolis

In general, city clothes should be trimmer, coats and suits less bulky. Shoes should be darker and more subdued. Strive for fairly simple silhouettes, more subtle tones, a more sophisticated look.

For evening, your clothes may be as glamorous and sophisticated as will suit your particular type of social life. If you are attending very festive events, dress accordingly. Choose from a wealth of fabrics, colors, and silhouettes that you may wear with assurance in the city.

For quiet dinners or the theater, wear a short dinner dress or dress-and-jacket cos-

tume in a soft brocade or silk damask. Most department stores now have ''after five'' boutiques.

For a Dinner Party

Wear the classic shirtwaist after-five-type dress with sleeves or jacket.

For At-Home Parties

Lounging pajamas are perfect, or a decorative skirt and top. Choose colors that go with the decor of your home. Be sure your clothes are comfortable.

For Club or Committee
Meetings

Be quietly and simply dressed up. Remember that you will be sitting most of the time, so wear something wrinkle free. Suits and dresses are best. Don't wear sparkly jewelry for daytime meetings.

Church Retreats

If the scene is ''woodsy,'' pantsuits are most appropriate. Wear casual attire.

Sunday A.M. Church Service

Wear a classic suit or simple dress. I personally believe that church is the place where you dress well, that a dress or a suit is better than pants. (And yet never look down on someone who isn't dressed as you are.) Certain attire makes us receptive to listening and respect as well. Sleeveless dresses and dangly jewelry do not belong in church. Be conservative but not dull, drab, or dowdy.

For Weddings

Guests Wear light-colored dresses and suits. If a dark costume is worn, brighten it with a gay accessory. It is poor taste to wear a very low cut dress. For a formal wedding in the evening, you may wear a long dress; for a daytime formal wedding, a street-length dress or suit. Hat and gloves are optional.

Are we putting the cart before the horse? What about the women in the bridal party? The size of your wedding, the location, the time of day, and the type of wedding are the determining factors of the style that is worn.

Informal Daytime and Evening Wedding

Bride Floor-length dress in white or pastel, or a suit or short dress. A bridal-type hat or a short veil. Select a corsage, prayer book, or small bouquet. Wear coordinating shoes and gloves.

Bridesmaids Wear the same length as the bride, or if she chooses a floor-length gown, you can still wear short dresses. Select accessories that are appropriate to the look.

Mothers Suits or street-length dresses.

Semiformal Daytime Wedding

Bride Floor-length dress in white or pastel. Elbow-length or shorter veil. Use formal wedding rules for accessories.

Bridesmaids Use same rules as the formal wedding, but fabrics and styles can be with less detail.

Mothers Use formal wedding guidelines.

Semiformal Evening Wedding

Bride Trim and fabrics can be more detailed and elaborate than semiformal daytime weddings, otherwise the same dress.

Bridesmaids Long evening gowns with the accessories the same as the semiformal daytime wedding. Fabrics can be more detailed and elaborate.

Mothers Use formal wedding guidelines.

Formal Daytime Wedding

Bride Ivory, white, or soft pastel (very delicately tinted) floor-length dress, a cathedral or sweep train. A long veil can make the train or cover it. If the veil is shorter, keep it very full with layers. Prayer book or bouquet. Gloves are optional, unless you choose to wear a short-sleeved dress, then use long gloves. Wear simple jewelry and shoes to match your dress.

Bridesmaids Floor-length gowns. Hats or caps should not be elaborate; veils or hats are optional. Shoes should match or closely blend to the color of the gown. Gloves should complement the sleeve length. The dress of the honor attendant may match or blend in with the color of the other attendants' gowns. Bouquet may be any style.

Mothers Three-quarter or floor-length dresses in simple styles. Small hats are optional. Gloves, shoes, and corsages should be complementary to clothing. Mothers should choose colors, styles, and dress lengths which complement each other.

Formal Evening Wedding

Bride If the wedding is held after 6:00 P.M., it is considered an evening wedding. The wedding dress style is the same as the daytime formal wedding. The fabric may be detailed and elaborate, and the sleeves should be long.

Bridesmaids Long gowns with accessories the same as daytime attendants. Fabrics can be more detailed and elaborate.

Mothers Floor-length evening gowns with small head coverings. Choose dressy accessories—furs, jewelry, and so forth.

All the above suggestions and guidelines are compiled to assist you, not to stifle you. So allow for freedom and know that they are subject to change.

For Funerals

Avoid gaudy clothes. Darker, earthy-colored clothes are appropriate.

For Conventions

Take a good quality dress, a perfectly fitting suit with two pretty blouses, and an attractive after-five dress.

For Business Events

Dress positively! Wear a suit that is businesslike and attractive. Skirt and jacket should be of the same color (or blending colors), and of quality fabric (wool or gabardine). Blouse should be of a soft fabric with a bow or softly tied neck style. A shirtwaist or simple sweater dress with a belt is acceptable. Pantsuits are all right, if appropriate, but only if they are very chic. Avoid big prints and bold colors. Tweeds are fine.

For Traveling

Choose rumple-resistant, comfortable, climate-changing clothes. Wear a loose coat over a casual dress, shoes large enough to allow for possible swelling of the feet, and carry a bag large enough to hold tickets, money, programs, and brochures. Bring extra nylons, comfortable gloves, and a hat or scarf to protect hair. (*See* chapter 13 for more travel helps.)

For Television Interviews

Wear an outfit that reflects your professional image. Try wearing clothing that will harmonize with the set (call ahead if possible). Solid colors in earth tones, and blues in medium tones are great. Avoid especially bright colors and excessive jewelry that clangs.

Makeup should be heavier than usual and with a powder finish to eliminate shine. Television studio lights tend to wash out face coloring.

Avoid plaids. I once had a guest on my show who appeared with a plaid jacket, a striped shirt, and a polka-dot tie. And he wasn't portraying a clown! Rather embarrassing to have happen on a show about beauty!

For Speaking Engagements

Wear an outfit that speaks of integrity and authority, such as a suit or dress in a solid color. Avoid pastels, reds, or any color that might be considered nonprofessional. Beige is very good for platform wear. If you are sharing the speaker's platform and program, a dark suit with a contrasting blouse would be a good choice. If you are speaking to a group of women in a medium-range age group and there are many homemakers present, a soft suit or soft classic dress would be the best choice. Strive for the conservatively elegant look.

For a Job Interview

Sell yourself by your appearance. Dress for the job you are trying to get. For an office job, wear a business suit. Hair should be clean and neat, nails freshly manicured, and makeup conservative. Choose shoes, nylons, and jewelry carefully. (Refer to chapter 12 on working clothes.)

Wear a classic jacket and basic skirt in tweed, or in a solid color, with a softly bowed or tied blouse in a complementary color. Second choice would be a simple quality dress in a good fabric and of a solid color. Wear simple gold jewelry (no dangles or bangles!), and a basic pump. Nylons are a must (in leg color), with no runs!

Fingernails should be well manicured, with no obvious fake nails or "claws." Polish should be light to medium in color. No chipped nails, please!

Don't forget deodorant, and use little or no perfume.

Remember, grooming should be *immaculate.* The decision as to whether or not you will be considered for the position will be made within a few seconds, so your first impression is very important. When you are confident that you are well dressed and well groomed, you can go for your interview with the self-assurance that will bring positive results!

For job interview

Back to Work in Style

She is energetic, a hard worker, and watches for bargains. She works far into the night.

Proverbs 31:17, 18

The other day I read that in the 1950s a typical American family consisted of a working father, a stay-at-home mother, and one or more children. This constituted 70 percent of all households. Today this "typical" family accounts for only 15 percent of American households. The growth of single-person households, working women, and single parents has turned our idea of the American family upside down.

In 1938, 75 percent of the population disapproved of a married woman who worked if her husband was capable of supporting her. Today only 26 percent feel that way.

The United States Department of Labor reports that half of all women sixteen years and over (47 million women) are working or looking for work.

The return of the American woman to the nation's work force has become the phenomenon of the decade.

This morning I went to the Image Improvement headquarters, where we train women to teach the Image programs. I was wearing a beige blazer, an ivory blouse, a tailored beige skirt, and sensible camel shoes. Does it sound dull? Not to me—I call it "success dressing."

There was a time when I only worried about having on clean underwear so I wouldn't be embarrassed during gym class! But now, surrounded by a wealth of information on how to dress to show that I am a serious and purposeful person, my emphasis lies elsewhere.

Do you greet each morning with dread, your closet suddenly transformed into a dragon instead of a friend? Do you ask yourself probing questions each morning? Is this dress too seductive? Is that suit too drab? Will this jacket show you are assertive, but not pushy? Will your shoes speak of washing clothes and cleaning ovens rather than a promotion to executive vice-president?

All of us want to look successful. We all want to look as if we belong in the working world, but in doing so we may have lost our fashion individuality. We seem to be educated "Barbie Dolls." We cling to our sensible suits, and hope they will carry us through the often chauvinistic business world. We live in fear that the boss will say, "Oh, no, lavender suit! Promotion denied!"

Now I agree that to dress so differently people feel uncomfortable or want to laugh out loud is self-defeating. But I refuse to believe that a woman's superiors will view her as unpromotable because she wears a lavender suit or blouse from time to time.

The success look

Times are changing? I hope so! Today our professional woman, although well aware of the need to dress appropriately, no longer feels the need to play it safe by putting on a uniform. She wants an authoritative look that reinforces rather than dominates her image. She knows that clothes don't make the total woman, and the right clothes are no substitute for hard work. She decides what works best for her and her style, and has a strong desire to express her individuality. She de-

mands durable, flexible clothing that takes her through workdays and into her after-hours without much fuss. Classic quality items give her years of mileage, and with a few new pieces and accessories, she can update her look easily and economically.

In this section you will find some good combinations for the look of success. They are go-with-everything, go-anywhere combinations that can be dressed up or down with blouses and changes of jewelry. (A suit is unsurpassable, effective, and can be very feminine—and still professional.)

Always keep in mind that *you* represent your company, organization, office, or group to the public. The impression you create may be the only one others see. You have an obligation to appear clean, attractive, and professionally well groomed. Impressions are lasting, and part of your salary depends on your grooming.

For dealing with the public

For the nonvisible-type job

Some Tips

Your first thought may be, *How can I dress for my company* and *for me?* And, *How can I wear a jacket during warm weather?* The answers depend on how much of your job requires that you deal directly with the public. If you are highly visible to the business world, you must look first-rate all the time. When the weather is warm, dress so that you can remove a jacket and still look professional. Choose the lightest weight, coolest fabrics. Do remember that blouses will look more sophisticated when tucked in rather than worn outside a skirt or pants.

Maybe your job doesn't require much public contact. Possibly you work in a "nonvisible" type job. If so, you will need comfortable, easy-care clothing to travel from appointment to appointment all day. Pants can be the answer, and they work especially well with a jacket. Worn together, they maintain the authority you need if you are in a supervisory position. Your best choices for a professional look are solid colors.

For the creative job

For the messy job

If you have a creative job, you can afford to be imaginative and flexible in your clothing. Yet, you don't want to alienate the more conservative businesspeople you may come in contact with. A sense of balance is necessary. Possibly your style may be classic but the colors you use will be innovative and unique. Color can often be used this way without looking too "way out." Many women in this position feel that they can wear one item of "signature" clothing (a piece of distinctive jewelry or a less than classic skirt in a strong color or print) and look great.

The most difficult "what to wear" problem faces the woman with a "messy" job—for example, the artist or printer who works with inks or photo copies. The job requires clothes that are wash-and-wear, and you can't afford inappropriate clothing. But unless you're actually out in a coal mine, or digging ditches, you shouldn't dress too casually. You'll not only look sloppy but you also may find that your work is not what it could be. The way you look affects how you feel about yourself and your job effectiveness. If you get careless with your clothing, your performance may get that way, too!

Guide to a Professional Woman's Wardrobe

One Skirted Suit The color will depend on the season and geographical area. *For summer:* a lighter-colored linen suit. *For winter:* a darker-colored wool suit. The suit style should be classic, to be worn with blouses.

Two Skirts Colors to coordinate with the skirted suit. The style depends on your figure type.

Four Blouses or Shirts Three solid colors, one small pinstripe. Open shirt collars or bowed blouses are best. Long-sleeved styles in silk or silk-look fabrics. All to coordinate with jackets and skirts.

Scarves These should coordinate with the above blouses. Menswear paisleys, stripes, solids, or polka dots in conservative patterns, ascoted at the neck. Wear contrasting colors such as a maroon ascot scarf with a white blouse and navy suit. Silk or silk-look fabrics.

Two Dresses Colors and styles that work with the jackets. Shirtwaist styles are excellent for the professional woman. Beige or taupe; solid colors are best. Never sleeveless. Long sleeves are the best buy. Add a jacket for professionalism.

One or Two Jackets or Blazers Solid colors, tweeds, or a very muted plaid to coordinate with all the above clothing. Wools or wool blends are excellent for winter. Linentype fabrics for summer. Wear a jacket when dealing with the public.

One Coat The classic trench coat, belted. Beige. Length to cover all skirt-length clothing (*see* page 98 for photo).

Two Pairs of Shoes Closed heel and toe pumps are the best. Medium heel. Closed toe, slingback shoe with a medium heel is second choice. Basic colors. The same color, or darker than the hem of your garment. Always all *leather.*

Hosiery Neutral shades. Always keep an extra pair in your desk or handbag for those emergencies.

Jewelry Conservative pieces—14k gold gives a quality look. Earrings are good, but it's best not to wear more than two pieces of jewelry at a time, excluding your watch. While this is a good guide for a businesslike appearance, some professions may require that you wear more.

Pants If pants *must* be worn, or are required, wear only a tailored pantsuit that fits well. Add a bowed blouse. Never be an "imitation" person by wearing a chalk or pinstripe. Skirted suits are still the best choice for a businesswoman.

Attaché Case Carrying a brown leather attaché case can be the extra that gives you a competent, businesslike look. Your wallet should be leather and should blend with the attaché case or your handbag.

Umbrella Umbrella should be in solid beige.

Suggested Styles for the Working Woman

Suggested wardrobe for the woman in management, business owner, leader, and all professional careers:

Jackets

Blouses/Shirts

Skirts

Dresses

Pants
(If you must wear pants, always wear them with a jacket.)

Suit

The clothing depicted below is not the attire for a woman who wishes to look successful and gain promotions in the business world. Surveys have proven that sweaters are not as effective as jackets. Sweaters, it has been said, are for file clerks, not managers or executive secretaries.

Suggested attire for a file clerk, schoolteacher, sports director, school counselor, youth worker, or social worker:

Tops

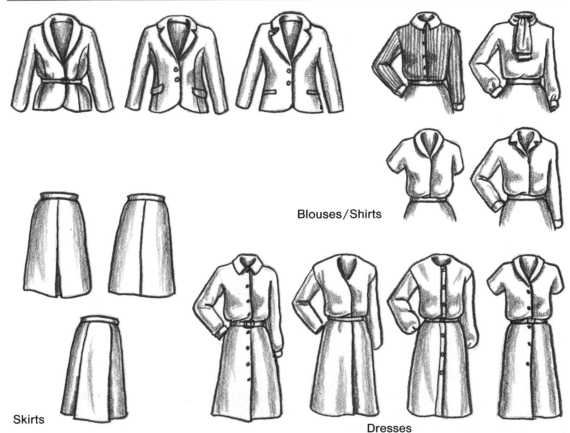

Skirts

Blouses/Shirts

Dresses

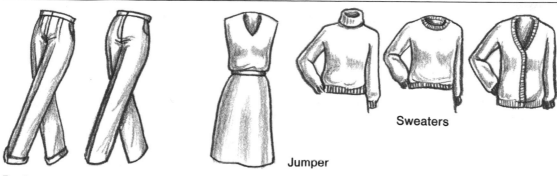

Pants

Jumper

Sweaters

Suggested wardrobe for a factory worker, production worker, repair worker, construction worker, or housekeeper:

Jackets

Sweaters   Blouses/Shirts

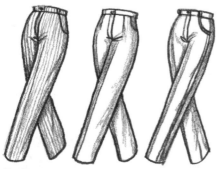

Pants

Tops

Finding a Versatile Working Dress

Color

The dress should be all one color, with no contrasting trim or topstitching. The color should be neutral. Bright colors will not interchange as easily as basics.

Neckline

The neckline should be adaptable to wearing blouses or tops underneath, or jackets over the dresses.

Best neckline samples are:

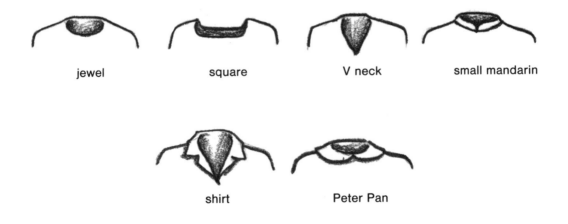

| jewel | square | V neck | small mandarin |

| shirt | Peter Pan |

Necklines which are not as versatile are:

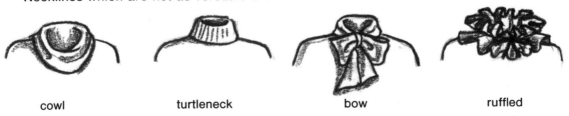

| cowl | turtleneck | bow | ruffled |

Sleeves

A working dress should not be sleeveless. A sleeveless dress worn over a blouse or sweater gives a jumper effect and a "junior" look. The best sleeve length is to the wrist. The sleeve should not be so bulky or wide that it won't fit into jackets, but wide enough to wear a blouse under. (Half-length or three-quarter-length sleeves are very limiting.)

Bodice

The bodice should have enough ease to accommodate layering of garments.

Straight cut, adjusted by belt

Elasticized waist

Fabric Insights

Year-Round Fabrics

lightweight jerseys
twills
challis
wool
gabardine
lightweight flannels
cottons (for shirts)
silk or silk look

Fabric Connotations in Business

wool, linen, silk: quality, taste, success
corduroy: too young, not proven yet, going to
    college
denim: "Don't take me seriously."
polyester: "inexpensive" (Unless a *fine* quality gabardine of the type used in suiting. A durable working-suit fabric may be 55 percent wool and 45 percent polyester. Polyester that looks like real silk is okay.)

cotton (broadcloth): Ivy League, influence, affluence
leather (in jackets): gangland
leather (handbags, attaché cases, shoes): success, quality
velvet: evening life

gold pens: success

The above notes may not apply to the fashion-career person or one who is not in the working or professional world.

How to Be Groomed for Success

Look neat, look successful, be an asset to your profession!

1. Don't let there be a clash in your image: look the same each day. The average person doesn't feel comfortable with drastic changes, so change your colors and/or fabrics, but not your general look (unless it needs improving!).
2. Bathe daily and always use deodorant or antiperspirant.
3. Use breath spray, mouthwash, or sugarless breath mints often.
4. Don't wear an excessive amount of perfume. None may be best.
5. Refuse to wear anything too tight, too low, too clinging, or that is see-through. Such items do not belong in the business profession.
6. Clean and press clothing often between wearings. Double-check often for body odor or spots. Remember that fluorescent lighting can bring out many spots in clothing.
7. Do not wear white shirts or blouses more than once without washing. Cuffs and collars are noticed first.
8. Check your undergarments to see that they are mended. Undergarments should not be visible when one is standing, sitting, or bending over. Double-check to see that your undergarment straps are secure and will not drop out on your arm. Never wear colored undergarments with light-colored clothing. Choose skin color for work.
9. If pants are worn, be sure you check fore and aft! Bikini panty lines should never be seen. And no polka dots under white slacks!
10. Be sure your slip is neither too long nor too short.
11. No thigh-high slits in skirts, dresses, or wraps that gap open when you sit.
12. Don't be careless about little things. Sew on buttons and snaps. Stitch up loose hems.
13. Check yourself in a full-length mirror before going to work. Be certain that no hem is hanging below your coat.
14. Do not wear jewelry that dangles, clatters, or distracts.
15. Underarms and legs should be clean-shaven.
16. Check to see that your nylons are not bagging at ankles or knees. Wash them out after each wearing.
17. If you are wearing a knitted dress, you may want to wear control-top panty hose to avoid bulges.
18. Never go without hose when dealing with the public. If you get a run, change to a new pair. Wise working women keep that spare pair handy for such emergencies.
19. Keep shoes polished and heels in repair.
20. Rotate shoes on successive days. This helps banish foot odor.
21. Apply makeup carefully and be sure there is no makeup line at the chin.
22. Hair is the frame of your face. Shampoo often (no dandruff on clothing). Get a good haircut every six weeks.

Hair should be of moderate length (no hair below shoulders, and avoid short styles that might be considered mannish). Consult hair charts for colors most flattering to you.

23. Hands should always be well manicured. Nails should not be extremely long or too brightly polished.

24. Glasses can add an authoritative look. Choose plastic frames in grays or browns to flatter your natural coloring. Avoid wire rims. Consult a glasses chart and choose frames in a style to complement your facial shape. Select a frame color no darker than your hair (lighter is best).

Appropriate Working Hairstyles

Hair care and style are discussed in chapter 17. Below are a few hairstyles that are good examples of appropriate hair for the office. It is best to keep the hair off the shoulders and always neat, clean, and professional.

A Travel Wardrobe

Take a duffle bag if you have one. . . .

Luke 22:36

Eastern Airlines statistics last year alone credited women with 28 million business trips. And those were *business* trips—not pleasure! Women are traveling for business *and* pleasure now more than ever before and, unfortunately, often enjoying it less.

147

Lost Luggage?

Have you ever had the unnerving, ungluing experience of arriving alone in a strange, large city, thousands of miles from the warm comforts of home, then heading for the baggage checkout area of the airline to retrieve your weary bags, only to find that your luggage was lost or stolen in Waukoganee? Where's that?

That happened to me! I was to address a VIP group of business representatives from various organizations, on the subject of success dress. They, in turn, had the responsibility of hiring or not hiring me for further engagements with their corporations. I had arrived very tired from a two-week speaking schedule, so had packed all my clothing, notes, and visuals in my suitcases! . . . It is now many months later, and not a sign of my bags. (I miss my worn-out Bible most of all!) The advice I'm about to give comes from a well-traveled person—please heed!

Note: I immediately bought a new suit of clothes, prayed a lot—and spoke anyway. Any professional knows that the show must go on—and I was hired, too!

Whether you travel one hundred or one thousand miles, planning is the key word, and when it's done right, it is all rather simple.

Let's Begin With What

to Wear

If you are a woman traveling alone, I suggest that you dress as if you are a successful businesswoman (even if you happen to be a housewife). Wear a suit look in a wrinkle-free fabric with a blouse. If the weather is cold, add a sweater.

Carry a large leather bag, over-the-shoulder style. In cold weather wear your boots, as this will save valuable packing space, and carry a coat with a warm zip-out lining. In good weather wear pumps.

What to Pack

It's wonderful to know you can take all the clothing you will need for at least a four-day stay, tucked in a small, crushable tote that will fit under the airplane seat or in the backseat of a car.

Here are the indispensables (use only one or two main colors):

2 silk-look blouses (in addition to the one you are wearing)
2 medium-weight sweaters in colors that will blend with all of the clothes you are taking
1 sweater cardigan vest to wear with the dress, over blouses, and with the suit skirt
1 pair of color-coordinating slacks
1 jersey dress of packable fabric in a solid basic color to coordinate with the suit jacket and other pieces
2 pairs of shoes (1 pump for walking and 1 sandal for day and evening)
jewelry in fashionable looks for day and evening
scarves, belts, and accessories for all of the above
1 shawl to throw over the shoulder of the jacket, or to be used as an evening wrap
underclothes, panty hose
nightgown
toiletries

How to Pack

Use the carryon—a soft, crushable "double duffle bag." (Use all the items listed in "What to Pack.")

Be sure your bag measures no more than eight inches high, sixteen inches wide, and twenty-one inches long, as this is the size of the areas under *most* airline passenger seats.

1. In the bottom of the bag place shoes and toiletries.
2. Roll all underclothes together inside the soft nightgown and tuck the roll on one side of the duffle bag.

buttons and stuff the sleeves with tissue paper to prevent wrinkles.

3. Three jackets can be hung, one on each hanger, over all other clothing. Place hair dryer and other accessories in your carryon bag.

Note: Never pack jewelry in bags that are to be checked, and never leave jewelry in your hotel room.

3. Roll up all belts and scarves tightly inside the shawl and place on the opposite side of the underclothes.

4. Put hosiery and jewelry in plastic zip bags and tuck inside shoes.

5. Place the jersey dress on the bed, face up with arms extended. Put the sweaters, blouses, and vest, one on top of the other. Take the right-side arms and cross them over the pile. Do the same with the left side so you have the arms all crisscrossed. Bring the hem of the dress up to make a fold in the center, and gently begin to fold the stack of clothes into three sections. Then place the clothes in the suitcase, all ready for the trip!

No baggage check needed! Your luggage arrives when you do, and there's no waiting!

The Garment Bag

This bag can take you through a two-week trip. It's all in how you pack. Layer three or four items on sturdy hangers.

1. Neatly fold two pairs of pants, then skirts, and a dress down the middle and and put on one hanger.

2. Layer blouses (one to four on a single hanger) on a second hanger. Button top

Clothing Checklist for Travel

My next vacation and/or travel will be on (date)_____
Location:_____
Weather:_____

I will pack these few articles of clothing to coordinate for my entire trip. (Use 2 or 3 main colors only.)
Color 1_____Color 2_____Color 3_____

Sweater (s):_____
Blouse (s):_____
Dress (s):_____
Jacket (s):_____
Top (s):_____
Skirt (s):_____
Coat:_____
Shoes:_____
Accessories:_____

Underclothes, lingerie:_____

Toiletries:_____

Extras:_____

I plan to take a ☐ suitcase ☐ duffle bag ☐ hanging garment bag

Clothing Care

No one tears off a piece of a new garment to
make a patch for an old one. Not only will the
new garment be ruined, but the old garment will
look worse with a new patch on it.

Luke 5:36

Saving money on clothes doesn't stop with
the actual buying. To truly get your money's
worth, you must not only take extra care in
selection but you must always take care of
needed repairs immediately.

You also need to learn which stains re-
spond to home remedies and which need
professional attention.

Develop updating skills so you can make
last year's purchase look like this year's
best-seller!

Recycling Clothing

Updating a Shirt Collar

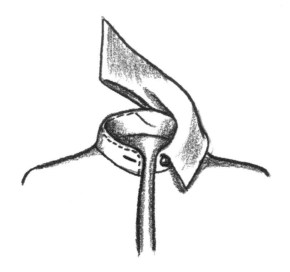

With a seam ripper, open the stitching line where the collar is attached to the collar band, and remove. Stitch the collar band carefully back together and presto! you have a new mandarin-collared blouse! I've kept many of these "removed" collars and put them back on blouses in another year of regular-collared blouses.

Changing a Neckline

Remove the collar and neckband to make a jewel neckline, or add a new collar of fabric or lace. Baste the new collar on the outside of the blouse with its edges just inside the old seam line.

Shortening a Jacket

If the jacket has patch pockets, remove them. If there is a lining, undo the lower edge and open out the front facing. Pin the jacket to the desired length, and cut the fabric and hem. Do not add the pockets unless the proportion is still correct. Belt the jacket for an updated look.

Add Braid Trim

Use fold-over braid to disguise worn edges of your jackets and suits.

Skirt or Pants Updating

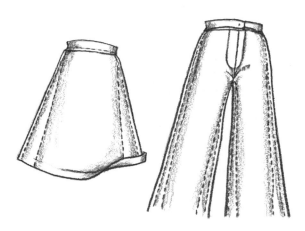

Turn the garment inside out and remove the hem. Ask a friend to pin out the excess fabric while you have it on. Make a seam with the pins. Always take equal amounts off both sides of the fabric. Use seamstress chalk and mark the new seam lines. Machine stitch, cut off excess material, and hem.

Buttons

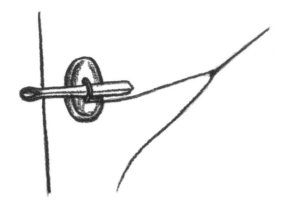

Remove old buttons and sew on new ones. Here's how to sew on a button so that it won't fall off or mar the fabric: Use regular or buttonhole-twist thread and knot the ends. Wax the thread with beeswax. Place the button in the correct position, begin sewing, but leave a "shank" by putting a matchstick or bobby pin on top of the button. Wrap the shank tightly with the thread. Then pull the thread to the wrong side and knot it.

Hemming

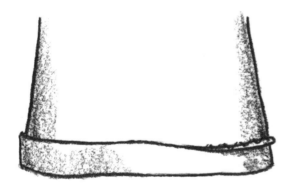

Fusible web (iron-on hemming tape) is the easiest way to put up a hem. But the couturier hem is the best way.

Ask a friend to pin your hem at the best length for you. Remove the skirt and finish the hem with pinking that is topstitched on your sewing machine; or sew on seam binding; or if it is a lightweight fabric, fold once and topstitch.

When the edge is completed, turn the hem up, then slip it back (as illustrated), and stitch in a zigzag pattern, catching one stitch in the hem edge and one stitch in the garment itself.

If a line shows from a let-down old hemline, try to remove the fold mark with a solution of white vinegar and water.

Preventive Measures

Stains and dirt wear out fabrics, so here are some helpful hints:

1. Save all "care" tags, extra buttons, and thread. Write on the care tag what the purchase was and keep it in a safe place. You may need the information at a later date.
2. Read clothing labels. Is it hand washable, dry-cleanable? Follow the label instructions.
3. Stains can be removed more easily from Scotchgarded clothes, raincoats, and canvas items.
4. Wear dress shields under dry-cleanable clothing. You'll save lots of money in cleaning costs.
5. Use a scarf or a model mask to keep from getting makeup stains on clothing when dressing.

Fur Storage

During the warm months, store your furs professionally in a vault as heat, humidity, light, and insects can damage fur or cause it to change color. Sales clerks at the store where you purchased your fur can recommend the best storage place in your area. The most common fur-storage months are mid-March through September.

Rabbit fur sheds, and there is nothing you can do about it. The shedding, however, is not enough to be noticeable in most cases.

Gadgets for Mending

Knit-pick Pulls snags through to the back side of knits. A marvelous device, and inexpensive.

Underwear Repair Kit Replaces straps and back fasteners when the elastic has lost its stretchability.

Sweater Comb An abrasive metal tooth that removes "balls" from sweater knits. Sometimes an emery board, used gently, will work in an emergency.

Iron-on Mending Tapes and Fusible Webs The answer for people who don't like to sew! Hems can even be ironed into place with fusible webs (such as Stitch Witchery).

Home Stain Removal

Stain removal can be hazardous to the fabric, so it is always best to let a professional remove stains; but if you feel you want to do it at home, try these ideas from my dry cleaner:

1. Test the effect of water or cleaning fluid on a seam before using on the garment.
2. Place a towel under the stain to absorb the water or cleaning fluid.
3. Never apply water to ink or lipstick stains, as this may release dyes and stain the fabric permanently.
4. Never try to remove stains from delicate fabrics.
5. Some fruit juices and drinks disappear into the fabric and leave no visible stain. Heat, however, will cause the "invisible" stains to turn yellow. This yellow stain cannot be removed. When you spill juice or a drink on your garment, flush it out promptly with water, or better still, take it to your dry cleaner.
6. Avoid applying heat to a fabric that is stained in any manner, as heat will set the stain.
7. Remove stains promptly. Some are stubborn and set permanently unless removed immediately. The warmth of a drawer or closet, or even heat from the body, can set stains.
8. Try a one-to-five vinegar-and-water solution for vegetable-based stains. Then rinse with clear water.

9. If it's an oil-based stain (cosmetics, paints, ball-point ink, many medicines), place a towel under the stain, use a solvent such as Carbona or Renuzit; blot, but don't rub.

10. After a stain has been removed from a garment, often a ring will be visible. Go back and "feather" out the stain by applying more solution to the ring, feathering at the edge until it blends.

11. For blood on a washable fabric, use cold water (hot water sets the stain) and mild soap.

12. Chewing gum: Put the article of clothing in the freezer. The gum will freeze and crack right off.

13. Nail polish: Remove with amyl acetate nail polish remover. (Do not use acetone.)

14. If you put a red scarf in the laundry and all your white shirts turn pink, run the white clothes through the wash cycle with Rit Color Remover. Use according to the directions.

15. If you get candle wax on a garment, put brown paper over it, iron, then peel.

16. For coffee or tea stains, soak clothes in cold water before washing.

17. Sometimes a pen mark can be sprayed with hair spray.

18. When you clean a two-piece outfit, always do both pieces at the same time. Otherwise, you'll have variations in coloring.

Recycle Checklist

The clothing that I must update and recycle is listed below. For a goal to be set and an accomplishment to follow, I have listed the ''goal date'' for the project to be completed. (*See* chapter 7 for closet cleaning.)

Item:_____
Changes to make:_____
Date I will complete this project:_____

Item:_____
Changes to make:_____
Date I will complete this project:_____

Item:_____
Changes to make:_____
Date I will complete this project:_____

Item:_____
Changes to make:_____
Date I will complete this project:_____

Item:_____
Changes to make:_____
Date I will complete this project:_____

Item:_____
Changes to make:_____
Date I will complete this project:_____

Note: *See* pages 88, 89, which state that if you don't update the clothing within twelve months, it is likely you never will so give the clothing away!

How to Dress the Man You Love

15

The intelligent man is always open to new ideas. In fact, he looks for them.

Proverbs 18:15

Joan, one of our Image Improvement teachers, received a phone call from her brother, Bob. He was looking for a new job and wanted tips for an upcoming interview. It was, he said, an executive job for which no one had been hired in the past who was less than thirty years of age. Bob was twenty-three.

"How badly do you want the job?" Joan asked.

"More than anything else," he replied.

"How much money do you have in savings?" asked Joan.

"I have exactly three hundred dollars."

"All right," said Joan. "Take the three hundred dollars out of the bank. Go to the most selective shop you can find. Buy the best navy wool suit, white shirt, and conservative tie you can find for three hundred dollars." She heard Bob gulp at the other end, but she continued. "Go to the library and find out all you can about that company. Then go prepared to look and act your best."

Bob went to the interview the following Friday at 9:00 A.M., prepared and looking the part of a successful executive. At 3:00 P.M. he was sent by plane to meet the president of the company. And he got the job—the youngest man ever to hold that position. Bob had had that professional look for those all-important first impressions.

Many men don't like to shop, and they ask their wives to do it for them. My personal opinion is that men should find a quality store and salesperson, learn to shop on their own, and leave their wives at home (unless the wife is a trained professional image consultant).

It's a proven fact that most women who shop for their husbands do so with an entirely different image of them than the working world has. Their purchases can sometimes actually be detrimental.

If I were not a trained wardrobe professional, a tie which I may select for my husband, Jim, might not be conservative or professional enough for his business image. (Jim is vice-president and executive director of our international Image Improvement Corporation, which trains consultants to become image specialists and teach our programs.)

In chapter 4, figure problems and solutions were discussed for women. A man must be just as aware of dressing with his particular physique in mind. How can you help?

You can make things easy on your man by clipping a small piece of fabric from the inseam of his trousers (or the remnant left after hemming his slacks) and gluing it to a 3" x 5" card.

On the card write the following information:

    Article of clothing:
    Date purchased:
    Fabric content:
    Price:

If he is looking for another piece of clothing to match, all he has to do is take the 3" x 5" card with him, and his ties, jackets, shirts, and so forth will all be the correct match.

> *Slacks purchased Mar. 10, 1981*
>
> *100% wool*
> *$45.00*

For the Man Who Is Too Short

1. Begin by accepting the fact that he is short. Then make sure he avoids outfits that "cut him in two," as this will make him look even shorter. Solid colors are best.

2. Vertical lines in both pattern and cut are best.

3. Make sure jackets and suit coats are exactly the right length. Legs appear shorter below a long jacket, and a very short jacket makes one appear even shorter. Vests are good, but he should never wear a long torso jacket. Plenty of leg should show.

4. On a three-button coat, only the middle one should be buttoned, never the top.

5. Watch shirt collars, and use nothing larger than regular. Best colors are white and light blue.

6. Shoulders should be padded, with a squared look.

7. He should wear heavy shoes such as wing tips, but avoid high heels.

8. Shoes should blend with dark pants, possibly be darker, but never lighter.

9. Neckties should be long and narrow, with a vertical design. (Four-in-hand knot is great.)

10. Jackets should have long, narrow lapels.

11. Pants should be slim cut, never cuffed. Make sure they are the proper length.

12. Belts should be the same color as pants, or a blended color.

Get him to stand and sit tall! He'll look great, and he can create the illusion of looking taller.

For the Man Who Is Too Heavy

1. No bright colors or bold patterns. Medium to dark will be his best colors and will make him appear slimmer.

2. Avoid nubby, bulky, heavy, or rough fabrics. Use gabardines and flannels.

3. Small-striped suits and vertical designs are good. Accent height to de-emphasize breadth. Herringbone weaves are flattering.

4. No double-breasted coats or vests.

5. Avoid the tight-fitting look. Slightly padded shoulders are best.

6. Coats should be *slightly* longer than the average.

7. Suits with tapered sleeves and trouser legs are slimming.

8. No cuffed pants; and be sure length of pants is correct.

9. Longer, pointed shirt collars are good.

10. He should choose lightweight shoes without decorations, avoiding anything that draws attention to weight at lower part of the body.

11. Vertical lines in ties are important, and be sure ties are long enough! (The four-in-hand knot is best.)

12. Small buckles and narrow belts are good. Large ones emphasize the waist.

13. Belts should be the same color as pants (or a blended color).

Clothes can camouflage excess weight, but good diet and exercise is the best solution! If he is satisfied with his weight, he should follow the above guidelines for a longer and narrower look.

For the Man Who Is Too Tall and Slim

1. He should wear coats that are broad through the shoulders and loose fitting at the waist. No tight clothes.

2. Double-breasted suits are wonderful.

3. Coats should be a little longer than the average.

4. No small, narrow lapels and collars.

5. Nubby weaves and bulky fabrics will make him look heavier. Gabardines, wools, and tweeds are good.

6. Patterns are helpful. Also plaids and checks will cut the vertical line that makes one appear slimmer and taller.

7. Full-sleeved sport shirts should be avoided, as they make the arms look too thin.

8. Ties should have horizontal patterns or stripes. (Full Windsor knot is best.)

9. No vertical stripes. Horizontal stripes, solid colors, or patterns in any garment are best.

10. Heavy, bulky shoes with thick soles are good.

11. Pants should be exactly the right length. They can be cuffed (or not), but should never be tapered or tight fitting.

12. Belts may be of a contrasting color to pants if clothes are casual.

13. Two-color combinations in jacket and pants are good.

He should never be guilty of slumping to make himself appear shorter. Most people will recognize what he is doing. Clothes, however, can make the difference. Remember, the primary purpose is to produce horizontal lines.

Now that you know what kind of clothes your man should wear, how do you help select a professional-looking man's wardrobe? Read on. . . .

Guide to a Professional

Man's Wardrobe

A budget-conscious man can build a durable and versatile wardrobe by investing in quality clothing. It is better to purchase one good quality suit rather than two or three of poor quality. Solid colors are best and should be selected within the same color family. Shirts, ties, and other accessories should be purchased with color coordination in mind. (*See* chapter 3 for color help.)

Two Basic Suits Solid colors (navy blue or gray) in wool or a good wool blend. For the authoritative look, a navy suit, white shirt, navy and white small-dot tie. For the personable "selling" look, a medium blue wool suit, white shirt, and a white, blue, and maroon diagonally striped tie.

One or Two Blazers Natural-shoulder blazers are appropriate for some business occasions and all informal occasions. Tweed or solid-color wool blends. Suit coats should not be worn with sport pants, or suit pants with sport coats. If a suit has several pairs of matching pants, this is acceptable, as pants wear out much faster than coats.

Two Pairs of Trousers Solid colors that blend with the blazers, in wool or wool-blend fabrics.

Ten Long-Sleeved Dress Shirts Four to six white shirts, one light blue, one end-on-end blue, one ecru, and one small stripe. Small check patterns or stripes that will coordinate with suits are acceptable. Wear only with a solid-color tie. Cotton or cotton-polyester blends. No monograms.

Ten Ties Silk or silk-blend ties are the best. A 100 percent polyester tie doesn't have the "success" look that silk blends have. Two solid-color ties, four regimental or rep (diagonal stripe), three silk foulards in small patterns, one small-polka-dot tie, and one subdued plaid. Wear a patterned tie only with a solid-color shirt or suit. No pastel or bright, gaudy ties. Eliminate all white ties.

Two Pairs of Shoes Wing tip and dress slip-ons for suits. Black shoes are the best buy. No white shoes or white belts. If a tan or camel suit is worn, tan or camel shoes should be worn. Brown suit with brown or black shoes. Black shoes with black, gray, or navy suits.

Twelve Pairs of All-Black, Over-the-Calf Socks Black socks with all dark shoes. With camel or tan shoes, only camel or tan socks. No white socks, except with athletic-type shoes.

Three Belts Classic styles in 1 to 1½ inch size. Same general color as pants. Simple, small buckle.

Jewelry Gold gives a quality look. Eliminate all neck chains, ID bracelets, and so forth. (And use a gold pen, not a twenty-nine-cent ball-point!)

Briefcase Brown leather. (Plastic says all the wrong things.)

One Classic Beige Raglan-Shoulder Coat Belted and below knee length.

Further Recommendations

1. Through testing, it has been found that the color brown is acceptable for suit colors from midwestern to western areas—not olive or drab green.
2. No gold or pastel suits.
3. No bright or dark-color shirts.
4. Shirt and suit need to contrast, but suit and tie should be darker than shirt.
5. Shirt-collar size should compare with tie width. Small shirt-collar sizes take a narrow tie.
6. Tie should be long enough to touch top of belt, with no shirt space between. Tie should never be longer than middle of belt.
7. No 100 percent polyester suits.
8. No leisure suits.

Appearance is one's image to the community, and tells how one feels about himself and how he views his profession.

Basic Wardrobe for the Student

or Blue-Collar Worker

1. One three-piece suit, solid color (navy blue or gray), in wool or wool-blend fabric.
2. One tweed cardigan sweater in wool, and one wool pullover.
3. One dress shirt in white or light blue. Eight sporty shirts in solids and plaids.
4. One or two pair of jeans. One pair of dressy slacks, three pairs of casual pants. (All pants should blend with shirt colors.)
5. Three ties: one solid, one regimental, one small plaid.
6. One short, warm jacket. (Optional: one classic, raglan-shoulder overcoat.)
7. Two pairs of shoes, one a dressy slip-on and one a casual loafer.
8. Dark-colored socks.

The Perfect Fit

There's more to proper fit than just sleeve length and inseam mesurements. Below are a few tips to help your man get the proper fit the next time he buys these ready-made garments.

Jacket   When trying on a new jacket, raise arms above the head, then bring them slowly down to sides. This settles the jacket onto shoulders and enables one to judge a good fit. If the fabric bunches in any area, this indicates possible collar problems.

Notice the back of the jacket. Vertical wrinkles or creases indicate the jacket is too large. Horizontal creases, too tight. The same rule applies to trousers. Diagonal lines along the back of a jacket indicate that the opposite shoulder is too low (a common problem). This can be corrected with padding.

Vest   A vest should fit smooth and close to the body, without the slightest sign of pulling or creasing.

Sleeve   Correct sleeve length (for jacket) measures five inches from the end of the sleeve to the tip of the thumb. Shirt sleeves should be approximately one-half inch longer than jacket sleeve. The total look should be balanced and in proportion to the rest of the attire.

Shirt Collar   This should be perfectly fitted but not too tight, and starched for neatness.

Trousers   The break in the trousers will depend on many things, such as the type of shoes being worn, and his height and weight. For a short or heavy man, a break probably should be avoided.

Pant cuffs should be between 1¾ and 2 inches. Generally a patterned trouser looks best with a narrower cuff, whereas fine wools (for winter) or linens and cottons (for summer) look better with a wider cuff. Trousers that are cuffed can also have a slight break, but this is optional.

Remember the vertical and horizontal crease rules, and also that the tighter the fit through the waist, seat, and hips, the worse will be the wrinkling of the crotch area. Frequent pressing can be time-consuming and take the life out of the trousers.

Shoe   The weight of the body is divided between each foot, with 50 percent on the heel, 30 percent on the big-toe area (or ball of the foot), and 20 percent on the little-toe area. Therefore, a wide toe box with sufficient height is important for proper weight balance. A narrow toe area squeezes the toes together, diminishing balance.

A heel higher than 1½ inches is too high. It shifts the body weight too directly onto the toe area. The heel should support the foot solidly from the back of the foot to the point under the ankle bone.

What to Wear Where

Often men are confused as to what they should wear when invited to social functions that demand "white tie" or "black tie," or even "formal" or "semiformal" dress. The following guide should help determine what to wear at different social occasions.

White-Tie Occasion

This, quite simply, demands the most formal outfit going, with the possible exception of the dress uniform of rear admirals and five-star generals. It means a tailcoat. Since a tailcoat is required very rarely, it should be rented, not bought.

Formal (Daytime)

Coat   Oxford gray cutaway, with plain or bound edges. Single-breasted with either one or three buttons and peaked or notched lapel, or double-breasted with peaked lapels.

Pants   Black and gray striped.

Shirt   White piqué with wing collar and stiff or pleated front.

Tie   Gray striped silk four-in-hand.

Formal (Evening)

Coat   Black tailcoat with satin or grosgrain lapels.

Pants   Same fabric as coat, with satin side stripe.

Shirt   Piqué front with wing collar and French cuffs.

Tie   White piqué bow.

Semiformal (Daytime)

Coat   Single-breasted oxford gray jacket.

Pants   Black and gray stripe.

Shirt   White, pleated front, spread collar, and French cuffs.

Tie   Gray striped silk four-in-hand.

Semiformal Black-Tie Occasion (Evening)

Coat   Black dinner jacket (also called a tuxedo). White, pastels, and so on, are appropriate from May to September, or throughout the year in tropical climates. Single- or double-breasted, notched or peaked lapels or shawl collar.

Pants   Black, with side stripe; or, if the tuxedo jacket is of a deep color other than black, pants can be matching.

Shirt   Pleated, tucked, or ruffled formal shirt in white, beige, light blue, or other gentle colors. Traditional collar and French cuffs.

Tie   Black satin, velvet, or grosgrain. The idea is to match the lapel facings.

A Man's Wardrobe Checklist

Profession:_____
Job description:_____
_____

People contact: ☐ yes ☐ no
Type of clothing needed:_____
_____

Select 2 or 3 solid colors to work with in your coordination:
1._____ 2._____ 3._____
Height:_____ Check one: ☐ short ☐ heavy ☐ tall and slim

Let's begin to coordinate: List colors and style/type of clothing you need to purchase or presently own that is correct, based on the information learned in this chapter.
Trousers:_____
_____
Jackets:_____
_____
Suits:_____
_____
Dressy shirts:_____
_____
Casual shirts:_____
_____
Casual pants:_____
_____
Coat:_____
Ties:_____
Shoes, socks, belts:_____

Over Forty and Fantastic

16

She is a woman of strength and dignity, and
has no fear of old age.

Proverbs 31:25

Recently I heard a woman cite all the signs
that say you're not getting any younger:

you have more bottles of moisturizer than
    acne medication in your medicine chest
when buying shoes, your priority is comfort!
one of your most important wardrobe items is
    your control-top hose!
the clothes you've kept for years are back in
    style

Are you looking for a magic wand to wave away the years or for a foolproof guarantee to double-cross Father Time?

Or perhaps you think, *Well, why bother? Why not grow old, gracefully or otherwise?*

It's important to realize that today's woman is very different from yesterday's. As a generation, we look younger than our parents did at the same age.

There was a time when you helped a grandmother cross the street. Now you follow her, often rather briskly. (I know, because I'm a grandmother!)

But what if you are not a grandmother who walks briskly? What if your mirror reflects a woman who has become matronly, dowdy, and unattractive?

It's never too late to change—never too late to improve your image. Let's begin to develop that "ageless" look. It can be done!

An ageless person looks capable, dynamic, vital, healthy, and contemporary. She updates her hair, her makeup, her clothes, *everything.* She reads books and magazines and becomes an expert on herself. She doesn't copy other women who may be confused about their images. She wears what becomes *her.*

I can remember when fashion and age were an easy equation. When one became older, clothes automatically changed.

But today, we see ourselves differently. Our appearance makes that statement. Age is no longer the determining factor in wardrobe dressing, but a guideline. More important than age is one's life-style, work, and the geographical location of one's home.

Regardless of age, *why* and *how* you wear *what* you wear is most important. Confidence and attitude counts more than age.

Never *overdress* when you are in your forties. The statement "less is more" means to not overdo *anything.*

It was recently stated in a fashion magazine:

> In your 40's you're established on many levels—career, and/or family life, in your individual pursuits—and there's no question about it, you're expected to look the part. But you've learned by now how to use clothes to your best advantage—with a definite style of dressing, with the ability to resist the passing whims and fads of fashion.

It is important to present a look that says to the world that you care about your body, posture, makeup, and hair. (Shorter hair, but not extreme, is usually better for this age.) Pay attention to what makes you feel good about yourself.

Not so long ago, forty was over the hill, and fifty was old. Now, with marvelous research in skin and cosmetic products, it's possible to look attractive and energetic at any age.

When learning to dress for over forty, strive for a total look—shoes, handbags, everything. Mature women are often seen with everything from the neck to the hem ideal for them, then everything above and below in a fifteen-year rut!

Use solid colors that are easy to mix, such as navy, beige, gray, a pretty plum, and rosy colors. Then put the soft, pretty shades next to your face. Wear darker colors in pants, skirts, and culottes. Chapter 4 will help you understand what to wear for your figure and chapter 3 will help you pick the best colors for you!

Do cultivate a particular look, and don't jump from one trend to another (even though that sometimes brings compliments!).

Dressing for Camouflage

If you can afford only one good suit, make sure it is single-breasted, in the most classic cut. The cut of the jacket is the most important feature to be aware of. Solid colors and tweeds can be combined with pants and skirts and dresses. A jacket or blazer worn with a well-made skirt will give you a stylish, suited look.

A single-breasted coat can be worn open or closed. It's much easier to work with than a double-breasted jacket and is more slimming.

A short double-breasted jacket can be difficult to work with. Some of them are made to be worn with a specific suit and cannot be interchanged with other pieces of clothing. You may find what you planned as your main "investment" piece is not as versatile as you first thought.

Don't be afraid to use color. A suit needn't be black or navy. Medium to lighter tones will make you look feminine and soften harsh lines.

Use only quality fabrics such as gabardine, silk, and wool which, while they are not inexpensive, still pay dividends in longevity and professional image. Select clothing that can be worn most of the year.

A basic suit should be livened up with accessories and touches of color such as a shirt or blouse, scarf, and jewelry in complementary colors. Keep attention toward the face.

Here are some ways to look younger . . . fast!

Weight   Slimmer bodies look younger and age more gracefully. But don't get too thin, as your skin must have enough fat to be supple. Do remember that fast weight loss will bring flabbiness. If you must lose more than five pounds, do it slowly and steadily to avoid sagging skin. Begin a good exercise program. Your younger-looking skin will thank you for it!

Glasses   Switch to new ones. Try lighter-color frames. If you wear bifocals, ask about the new "no line" single-vision lenses. Check with your eye doctor about contact lenses.

Posture   Stand tall. Good posture can take years off your looks.

Dress Appropriately   Dress with your age in mind, but don't be dowdy. Don't use too many dark colors. Perk everything up with pretty accessories.

Hair

I'm often asked the question "Should I cover my gray hair?"

Sometimes this can be a mistake, as nature uses gray to soften face lines and skin tones. Coloring, however, may be a good idea for you, but a variation should be used for highlights. Chapter 3 will help you with questions regarding hair color for your skin coloring.

For dull hair, vitamin B, via a B-complex capsule, and avoiding the B-vitamin depleters such as caffeine, sugar, alcohol, and stress, will help.

Get a good cut at regular intervals. Short hair is more youthful than long, but a very short cut can be too severe. Softness around the face is good. You can wear a variety of styles, even a curly "wash and wear" if your hair is three or four inches long.

Your hairstyle can make you look five to ten years younger or older, depending on the style! Drab, unstyled hair, tight curls, "little girl" bangs, tight buns, tightly molded curls, garish hair colors, and teased hair all scream, "Dated!"

A face-framing style in a soft look is youthful. If your hair is mousy looking or unattractive as it grays, choose a color that's a shade or two lighter than your natural color. Colors such as jet black, flaming red, and platinum blond will age you even more. You may want to give your whole face a natural uplift by letting the hair be lightened around the face, blending to your natural shade at the nape of the neck.

Some gray hair is very beautiful and most flattering to the wearer. Your hairdresser will be honest with you, so listen to his or her suggestions.

Skin Care

Skin care is important for the woman over forty. Someone once said:

> At age twenty you have the face that God gave you.
> At forty you have the face you are working on.
> At sixty you have the face you deserve.

Two basic things happen to a woman's skin as she gets older: it gets drier, and it doesn't slough off surface cells as rapidly as before.

Cleanse your face for one to two minutes daily to loosen makeup and impurities, then add a little additional cleanser, and massage with a circular motion (light touch) to loosen dead cells and stimulate circulation. Apply a toner and freshener to remove residue and tighten the skin.

Don't be afraid to wear the creams and blushes and lipsticks (and even false eyelashes!) that make you look healthy. The biggest color mistake in makeup is the use of turquoise blue shimmery eye shadow. Blue tones usually should be avoided (blue eye shadow, blue pink lipstick, bluish blushers). True reds, pinks, coral, bronze, and golden tones (depending on your color season) will counteract sallowness. Earth tones sometimes give an older woman a washed-out look. Add color to your face, but be subtle.

There are two kinds of makeup: *fashion* and *corrective*. The rule for corrective makeup is that "whatever you do shouldn't look like you did it!" Fashion makeup is part of an overall statement that you are making. All makeup must begin with foundation for that beautiful effect, but it should look sheer while still doing the corrective work. (A professional makeup artist, available through our Image Improvement classes, can be of help to you in this area.)

A few more ideas for helping your skin look younger: Use a night cream every evening on your face, and a weekly face mask. This will do wonders.

Facial Exercises to Help Tone and Tighten Your Face

Many stage and television personalities use facial exercises to help retain their youth and beauty. Here are a few from the beauty experts for you to consider.

Mouth-to-Chin Furrows

Lift lower lip into a "pout" position.

Pucker lower lip. Bring both corners toward center.

Relax and repeat five times.

Frown Lines

Look straight into a mirror.

Try to bring eyebrows to center of your face.

Lift eyebrows as high as possible. Do exercise five times.

Double Chin

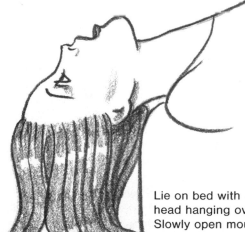

Lie on bed with head hanging over. Slowly open mouth.

Slowly close mouth. Repeat ten times.

How to Turn Back the Clock

You can look ten years younger in a matter of hours—and without a face-lift!

Look at yourself—really look at yourself. Are you still wearing makeup shades that were flattering to you ten years ago but are too bright and dated today?

Softness is the key for a younger look— soft makeup colors applied with a gentle but expert hand.

Begin with moisturizer, which is a must for all women, especially those over thirty years of age. Skin loses its ability to retain moisture as it ages.

Always use a water-holding moisturizer. Splash water on the face, and while it is still damp, apply the moisturizer. Otherwise the moisturizer will be of no benefit to you. Most women forget this most important step.

For foundation, try a lighter or liquid makeup base, preferably in a water-based brand. Skin tends to darken as we get older, so select a shade with a slightly rosy, peachy, or pinkish hue (depending on your color season); but choose a shade that is close to your own skin tone, perhaps just a shade darker. Blend carefully at the throat and neck areas.

To cover dark circles or puffs under the eyes, use an undereye makeup in a tone two shades lighter than your regular foundation color. The rule to remember is the lighter shade goes on the dark-circle areas, and the darker shade on the puffy areas.

Blush, if correctly applied, can make you look ten years younger! Smile, then dot cream or a liquid blush on the little "apples" of cheeks, blend cream up and out toward the temples. Avoid red or other bright shades. Again, rose, peach, or pink are the shades to use for younger-looking skin. Powder blushers tend to accentuate wrinkles and lines.

To finish the look, fluff translucent powder all over the face, brush off the excess, and then pat your face with a damp "sea sponge" to set the skin and make it look fresh.

Eye makeup should be soft in color and should complement your eye color and whatever you are wearing. Blend shadow from base of the lashes upward and out toward the end of the brow. Eyeliner, too, can be youthful if you select a soft shade (never black) and wing it up and out. Smudge it slightly with your fingertips or a cotton swab to blur the line and make it look more natural. Add a light touch of mascara in a medium or light brown.

As a former professional model, I can offer one tip that I always use for brightening my eyes: blend a tiny dot of white eye shadow near inner eye corners.

Penciled-on, harsh eyebrows are unnatural looking and aging. Use short, soft strokes. Select a light brown pencil, unless your hair is very dark. Always use a "lift" motion at the end of the eyebrow, and avoid exaggeration. Your eyebrows should not look like question marks or slants. Use your natural line and proceed with caution.

If your lipstick seems to bleed, use a moisturized lipstick to help minimize the lines; or apply foundation to lips, then lightly powder over them before using a lip pencil liner to softly outline the line of the lips. Lipstick will then have a dry surface to stick to. When lining the lips, don't forget to line the corners in an upward stroke. Remember that "upward" always means "young." Appealing and youthful lip colors include soft pink, rose, coral, apricot, and peach shades (depending on your season color).

The Externalities

> Your beauty should not be dependent on an elaborate coiffure, or on the wearing of jewellry or fine clothes. . . .
>
> 1 Peter 3:3, 4 PHILLIPS

The finished look in dressing with style can never be complete without attention to skin, hair, and good grooming from head to toe. Correct makeup, hairstyle, wardrobe, and grooming can help you project a lasting beautiful impression.

It goes without saying that good grooming should be as important to you as heat is to the occupant of a forty-degree house!

Good grooming begins with developing good habits. Pages 144, 145 gave many helps to all women who want to present themselves in a positive light. The necessities include a daily bath, deodorant or antiperspirant, underarms and legs cleanly shaven, undergarments mended and clean, nylons without runs and fitting well, shoes in polished condition and heeled. Also necessary are hemlines that are even, garments ironed and free from soil, hands and nails immaculate, with no chipped nail polish, clean hair with no traces of dandruff, and makeup that is well blended without any masklike effect or makeup line at the chin.

I personally believe in modesty and tastefulness, which means no see-through garments or thigh-high skirts. This can be accomplished with an up-to-date look in fashion and yet not compromise any of your standards.

A touch of class includes correct posture, using positive body language with graceful movements—yet not contrived. A complete lack of spontaneity in a woman is unbecoming and can destroy elegance.

The Image of Loveliness book will be a great additional source to help you acquire more of these positive qualities.

When deciding on a new hairstyle, keep in mind your facial features and shape. Here are some guidelines to follow:

Shape It Right

Round faces should be lengthened, or at least not shortened. Therefore the coiffure should have more height than width. Bangs that form a horizontal line across the forehead shorten and widen the face.

Round

Wrong

Right

Diamond

Wrong   Right

Pear Shaped

Wrong   Right

Square

Wrong

Right

Coiffures with height, arranged unevenly, are flattering to square faces, especially if the silhouette tapers inward at the top. Variety in line and a not-too-tight arrangement on forehead are best.

Coiffures that are widest below the temple are best for the heart-shaped face. On hair that falls below the hairline, bangs should form curved lines on the forehead.

Heart Shaped

Wrong

Right

Long Oval

Wrong   Right

Use a hairstyle that is widest in the middle of the head for this face. Usually a symmetrical coiffure without irregularities is best.

The Perfect Oval

This face is said to be ideal, so everything you do with coiffures, makeup, and necklines should tend to make your face look more oval.

Take a good, hard look at yourself. What do you see? Are you making errors with your hairdo? If so, you should know what to do to correct them.

Very few women are natural beauties. We all have imperfections, but why accent them? There are definite right and wrong ways to style a coif to suit your particular facial structure, age, and hair quality.

About Face

How do you create the illusion of a lovely face? As in everything else, it's easy when you know how! Begin by checking the one facial pattern that best describes your face shape.

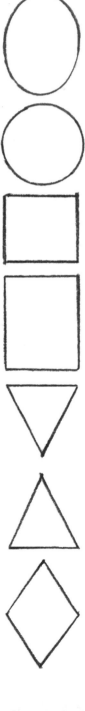

The Oval Face

Considered the perfect face shape. The contours and proportions of the oval face form the basis for modifying all other types. It is about one-and-a-half times longer than its width across the brow; the forehead is slightly wider than the chin. *Strive to maintain this oval contour.*

The Round Face

Round jawline and round hairline. *Work to create the illusion of length.*

The Square Face

Square jawline and straight hairline. *Work to create the illusion of length and offset the squareness in the jawline.*

The Oblong Face

Hollow cheeks and a long, narrow face. *Work to create the illusion of width and shortness.*

The Inverted-Triangle Face

Narrow chin and wide forehead. *Work to increase the width of the lower part of the face, and to narrow the width of the forehead.*

The Triangle Face

Wide jawline and narrow forehead. *Work to lengthen the face and create the illusion of width in the forehead.*

The Diamond Face

Extreme width through the eyes and cheekbones; narrow chin and forehead. *Work to diminish width across the eyes and cheekbones.*

Laying the Foundation

Beauty isn't instant—it's a *habit*. Skin care is the basis for a beautiful complexion, good grooming, and a healthy skin. Laying the foundation must come first. Here are the good habits of skin care:

Cleansers

use twice daily
products should remove makeup, oil, and
    impurities

Stimulants

scrubs for cleaning out impurities
masks for occasional skin toning and deep
    cleansing

Fresheners

for picking up residue from cleansers or stim-
    ulants
prepare pores to accept moisturizer

Moisturizers

give protection
replenish lost moisture
plump cells (for fewer wrinkles!)
give body for makeup
keep dirt out of pores

My first book, *The Image of Loveliness*, will give you additional advice on skin and hair care. If we have an Image Improvement consultant in your area, she will be the expert to see.

Makeup is *not* a cover-up—its purpose is to *bring out* your beauty!

Makeup Magic

Placement of shadow for a large nose:

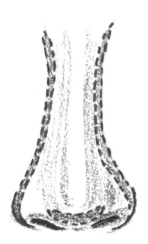

Highlight

Use *highlight* to straighten crooked nose, lengthen short nose, or make wide nose thinner. Keep off bumps or hooks.

Highlight and Shadow Areas

Use *highlight* for too-narrow, *shadow* for too-wide forehead and temple areas. (Diagram demonstrates one side of the face.)

Use *highlight* for eyes that are too deeply set or are sunken.

Use *shadow* for protruding orbital bone.

Use *highlight* under eye.

Nose: *shadow*.

Use *highlight* on laugh line.

Jaw: *shadow*.

Use *highlight* for shadow under lower lip.

Chin: *shadow* or *highlight*

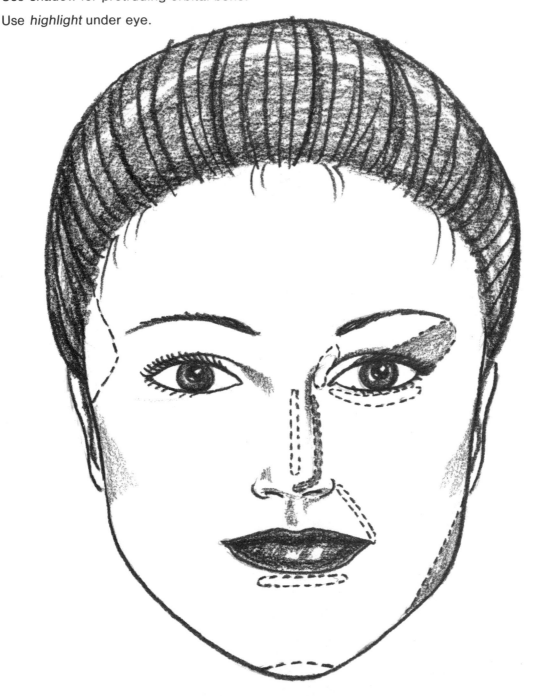

Jawline

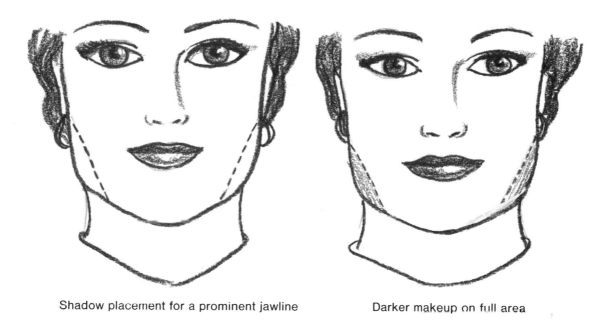

Shadow placement for a prominent jawline

Darker makeup on full area

The Eyes

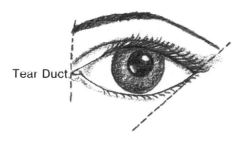

Tear Duct

The line of the eyebrow begins opposite the tear duct. Tweeze all hairs between the eyes. (Use an imaginary line up from the tear duct as a guide.) Shape your eyebrows from the inner corner of the eye, curving it with the eyelid open.

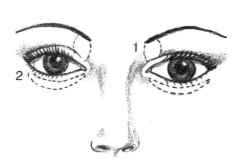

Highlighting areas for circles under the eyes (2); and deep-set eyes (1)

Indicate on this sheet all the areas of your face that need corrective makeup.

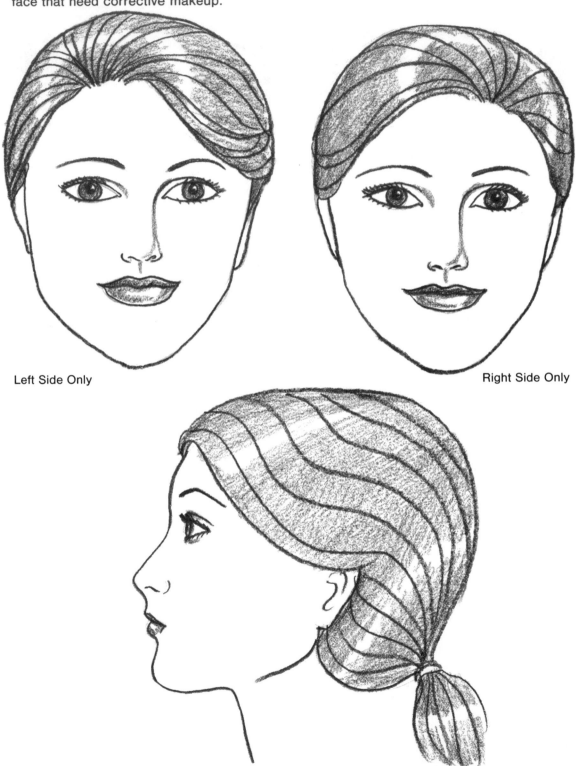

Left Side Only

Right Side Only

Side View

Glamour Items and Color

To help you select your best colors in makeup and glamour items, look on your color chart in chapter 3. The colors found on your season chart are the colors to follow for glamour colors in makeup. For example, a Cool Summer's colors include a mauve or a dusty rose. These would be good eye colors for her. If you have blue or green eyes and select an eye shadow color *brighter* than your eye color, it will appear as though your eyes are washed-out or faded in color intensity. Not following the proper advice can make you appear tired, depressed, and sallow.

Cool Summer Makeup Colors

Foundation   Rose, sand undertone base

Rouge   Rose, pink blue, burgundy

Eyes

Eye Color	Shadow Color
Blue	Ash blue to gray turquoise
Green	Ash or gray greens

(Wear darker shades on the orbital bone.)

Mascara and Liner   Charcoal, brown, taupe. Choose the color that is closest to the color of your brows and hair, without going lighter.

Eyebrows   Taupe, soft brown, without yellow or red in it

Lip Color   Rose, pink, plum, and burgundy

Nail Color   Rose, pink, plum

Cool Winter Makeup Colors

Foundation   Rose, sand undertone base

Rouge   Rose, blue pink, burgundy, real red

Eyes

Eye Color	Shadow Color
Brown	Gray navy, mauve, gray plum
Green	Ash to gray green
Blue to aqua	Gray turquoise, navy, ash blue, mauve

(Wear darker shades on the orbital bone.)

Mascara and Liner   Brown black, brown. Select the color which is closest to the color of your brows and hair color, without going lighter.

Eyebrows   Charcoal or brown. Do not use any red.

Lip Color   Pink, plum, burgundy, blue red, true red

Nail Color   Plum, true red

Warm Spring Makeup Colors

Foundation   Light to dark peach, ivory, basic beige, and all-yellow undertone base

Rouge   Coral, peach

Eyes

Eye Color	Shadow Color
Brown to amber	Golden brown
Blue to aqua	Soft turquoise and aqua
Green	Soft yellow green

(Wear darker shades on the orbital bone.)

Mascara and Liner   Light brown to rust brown. Select the color which is closest to the color of your brows and hair color, without going lighter.

Eyebrows   Golden to reddish brown

Lip Color   Peach, coral

Nail Color   Peach, coral

Warm Autumn Makeup Colors

Foundation   Ivory, peach, basic beige, and all-yellow undertone bases

Rouge   Brick, russet, nutmeg, deep peach

Eyes

Eye Color	Shadow Color
Brown to amber	Brown, copper, golden to darker brown
Green	Yellow green, brown
Blue to turquoise	Smoked turquoise

(Wear darker shades on the orbital bone.)

Mascara and Liner   Brown black to brown. Select the color which is the closest to the color of your brows and hair color, without going lighter.

Eyebrows   Dark brown to reddish brown

Lip Color   Coral, orange, rust, brick, peach, brown

Nail Color   Coral, brick

Skin and Hair Checklist

My face shape is:_____

My best hairstyle is:_____

Changes that I will make in my hairstyle are:_____
_____

My best makeup foundation color is:_____
My best rouge color is:_____
My best eyeshadow color is:_____
My best mascara color is:_____
My best eyeliner color is:_____
My best eyebrow color is:_____
My best lipstick color is:_____
My best nail color Is:_____

Changes that I will make in my makeup color and application are:_____
_____
_____
_____

Additional notes:_____
_____

Is That All?

. . . Clothe yourself with this new nature.

Ephesians 4:24

To think that I could write a book on wardrobe and mislead you to believe that clothes are all one needs to achieve happiness and success is to never be able to hold my head up high again in public. My every breath bursts with—BUT THAT'S NOT ALL!

Life with coordinated wardrobes and carefully organized closets filled with glorious accessories and clothing is marvelous, but unless the person *inside* all that outward splendor also changes and grows more beautiful, life can be intolerable, and terribly frustrating.

"Your beauty should not be dependent on an elaborate coiffure, or on the wearing of jewellry or fine clothes, but on the inner personality—the unfading loveliness of a calm and gentle spirit, a thing very precious in the eyes of God" (1 Peter 3:3, 4 PHILLIPS).

Only when I accepted the fact that I was made in the image of God did I start on the long road toward being a happy, confident, and lovely person to others. Only when I asked God's forgiveness through faith in Christ did I begin to really have the answers.

When opening my suitcase after returning from a conference in Hawaii, I found a fragrant lei which had been tucked in the corner with my clothing. The glorious aroma left a lovely fragrance which permeated my clothing. For weeks, I was aware of its perfume. May the sweet fragrance of the Christ permeate all that you do, so that you become beautiful from the *inside out!*

Joanne Wallace

Index